50

make-ahead baby & t

500

baby & toddler dishes

nutritious make-ahead recipes for meals for baby's first
foods through the toddler stage

Beverley Glock

SELLERS
PUBLISHING

A Quintet Book

Published by Sellers Publishing, Inc.
161 John Roberts Road, South Portland, Maine 04106

Visit our Web site: www.sellerspublishing.com
E-mail: rsp@rsvp.com

ISBN: 978-1-4162-0635-4
Library of Congress Control Number: 2011921887
QTT.BTFO

This book was conceived, designed, and produced by
Quintet Publishing Limited
6 Blundell Street
London N7 9BH
United Kingdom

Food Stylist: Nikki Gee
Photographer: Ian Garlick
Art Director: Michael Charles
Editorial Assistants: Sarah Quinlan, Holly Willsher
Project Editor: Anya Hayes
Managing Editor: Donna Gregory
Publisher: Mark Searle

10 9 8 7 6 5 4 3 2 1

Printed in China by 1010 Printing International Ltd.

contents

introduction

Weaning a baby can be daunting, especially for a new parent. When should you start feeding solids? Which foods should you give your baby? Which foods should you avoid? How much should you give? What texture should the food be? The questions go on and on, and you suddenly realize that breast or bottle feeding is actually very easy.

500 Make-Ahead Baby & Toddler Dishes will help answer those questions while inspiring you with simple, nutritious recipes for babies from their very first foods right through the toddler years. By making your own baby food, you'll save money and you'll know exactly what you're feeding your child, not worrying about checking ingredients on commercial baby food labels. Most of the recipes in this book are designed for the whole family to eat, so everyone eats the same meal, making your life easier.

ages & stages for solid foods

It's very important to introduce solid foods to your baby gradually and at the right time in their development. So read this section carefully and talk to your pediatrician if you have any questions. Also, read the section on food allergies and foods to restrict (pages 13–19) as well as the information on the "four-day rule" on page 8.

NEVER leave babies or toddlers on their own when they are eating. It is easy for them to choke on food or put it in inappropriate places such as ears and noses, so make sure that a responsible adult is always with them.

baby's first foods (4–6 months)

Do not give solid food to babies under 4 months, as their digestion is not ready and they should be wholly fed on breast milk or formula.

The recommended age to begin weaning is around 4–6 months; each baby is different and some are ready for solid food earlier than others. You need to trust your instincts and watch for signs from your baby that he or she is ready for some solid food. If your baby has been sleeping through the night and then starts waking up during the night demanding food, or begins drinking more breast milk or formula and does not seem satisfied, it may be time to introduce a little solid food. Always check with your pediatrician first.

Other signs of readiness to look for are:

• good head control

• trunk stability, able to sit alone in a high chair

• starts to reach for your food

• ability to swallow foods without gagging

Even when you've introduced some solid food, breast milk or formula should still be the primary food you give your baby.

Begin with one teaspoonful, once a day, of a solid food, usually rice cereal mixed with breast milk or formula, which is easy to digest. Once your baby has successfully eaten this for four or five days, with no adverse reaction, you can introduce a single fruit or vegetable. Wait for four days before introducing another. This is called the "four-day rule." By introducing one new food at a time, you can determine if your baby has an intolerance or allergic reaction to that food. Once you know which foods your baby enjoys and can safely eat, you can keep feeding them to your baby as well as trying new ones too. Work up to an ice cube-size (or 1 ounce), which is a portion for a young baby.

The food should be very pureed and have a sloppy, liquid consistency. If needed, add breast milk, formula, or the cooking liquid to the puree to achieve this very thin consistency. Young babies may have problems eating thick purees and may gag on them.

moving forward (6–9 months)
At this stage, babies can now eat virtually the same food as the rest of the family, but without any salt and more mashed than the adults. Begin to gradually introduce new flavors by using small amounts of herbs and spices. Make sure you check that all the ingredients are recommended for the age of your baby and omit any from the adult meal that are not suitable. Your baby will grow up knowing that children and adults eat the same food and everyone eats together. This goes a long way to prevent fussy eaters.

You'll still puree or mash the food, but it'll be a thicker puree than before. Keep portions based on 1 cube (1 ounce), but now introduce solids to more than 1 meal per day. If the

recipes calls for, say, one banana: a 6-month-old baby cannot eat a whole banana, but he or she would eat up to 1/4 mashed. The rest of the puree can be refrigerated or frozen.
Breast milk or formula should still be the baby's main drink up to the age of 12 months. You may give fruit juices in very small amounts — no more than 1/4 cup for babies under the age of 12 months. Juices must be 100% pasteurized fruit or vegetable juice, definitely not a fruit drink or juice drink. Juice should always be given from a cup, and not from a bottle. A bottle keeps the juice in contact with the baby's teeth for longer and can cause cavities.

At this stage, you can introduce dairy products such as yogurt, cream cheese, crème fraîche, and pasteurized cheese. These should be full-fat dairy products, because children under the age of 2 years need a diet that is 40–50% fat. However, do not give babies under 12 months cow's milk as a beverage or even in cooking. (Read more about dairy products on page 14.)

Eggs can be introduced if they are thoroughly cooked; scrambled eggs and omelets are good. Meat, chicken, turkey, and fish can be added at this stage. Start with milder flavors, such as chicken and white fish, before introducing beef, lamb, or salmon, so your baby has time to get used to new textures and flavors, before you gradually add stronger flavored food. Always mash the meat or fish first, and offer separately from a vegetable or mixed together, depending on your baby's preference. Make sure you add liquid to make it easier to swallow.

baby-led weaning
When your baby is 6 months and older, you could consider baby-led weaning, which means moving straight to finger food and allowing babies to feed themselves. No pureeing, no

mashing, no tiny baby spoons. Whether you go this route depends on when you wean your baby, as baby-led weaning is not suitable for babies under 6 months old. It also depends on you as a parent and whether you prefer the traditional method of pureeing and mashing the food your 6-month-old eats.

My personal preference is the traditional method combined with the introduction of some soft finger foods. The World Health Organization suggests that babies should be fed pureed food at the beginning of weaning as well as being given some finger foods. Baby-led weaning can be very messy, food ends up on the floor, there can be a lot of waste, and it is quite difficult to determine exactly how much food your baby has eaten.

If you choose to follow baby-led weaning solely, you will have to make sure that the food you give your baby is not too slippery to hold, as they will have difficulty and become frustrated. This could lead to fussy eating. So grind up cereal such as Cheerios or rolled oats to a powder and use it to coat tofu, mango slices, or any other food that is difficult to hold. Also, the food should be soft and chunky, as babies don't develop a pincer grip until after 6 months and will need to hold their food in their fist. Foods like broccoli florets and toast fingers are ideal.

eating with the family (9–12 months)
By now, babies are starting to assert their independence, holding forks and spoons and feeding themselves, although a lot of food will miss their mouths. Milk teeth may be coming through, making it easier for babies to bite. It's time to introduce textures and different

colors, so don't puree their food quite as much. Still, be very careful to give them nothing they can choke on. Stay clear of whole grapes, whole berries, cubes of hard fruit and vegetables and other hard food until children are over 3 years of age, as they are a perfect shape and size for children to choke on. You can, however, cut foods into very small pieces so babies can handle them better, and they won't become lodged in their windpipe.

toddlers (12 months & up)

Regularly introduce your toddler to new foods and new flavors. Take toddlers to the supermarket and let them choose a different fruit or vegetable to try each week. They'll feel they have more control over their food. Food doesn't need to be bland; in fact, the younger you introduce children to new flavors, the less fussy they'll be as they get older.

As soon as toddlers show an interest in cooking, let them help. If they can stand unaided and hold a spoon, they can participate in the kitchen. Toddlers enjoy stirring — even if they just have their own bowl and copy you when you're stirring — and they enjoy using their fingers to help you "rub in" the fat and flour to make gingerbread, biscuits, and thumbprint cookies. You'll be introducing them to a skill that will last a lifetime — cooking.

Watch out for how much sugar they eat (toddlers will love everything sugary!) and keep their juice intake to no more than 2–4 ounces a day of 100% juices, not juice drinks. Milk is still the best drink for toddlers, and it can now be cow's milk.

food restrictions

For various reasons, some foods are unsuitable for babies of certain ages. They fall into the category of "forbidden foods" or "restricted foods."

Remember, it's always advisable to check with your pediatrician before starting your baby on solid food. Also, if there is any family history of food allergies or intolerances, it is definitely best to consult your pediatrician regularly while introducing new foods to your baby.

Always remember the four-day rule when trying out new foods. That is, introduce them one at a time and wait for four days to see if there has been any reaction before you introduce another new food. This will help you determine if your baby has any allergies or intolerances to individual foods.

What is the difference between a food allergy and a food intolerance? An allergy is when the body mistakes a food for a dangerous invader and tries to expel it. To do this, the body produces antibodies, which in turn release chemicals called histamines. When histamines are released, the body produces symptoms such as runny nose, itchy eyes, redness around the mouth, rashes (similar symptoms to hay fever, which is an allergic reaction to pollen).

Very occasionally an anaphylactic reaction can occur, which is potentially life-threatening. If this happens, call for an ambulance immediately to go straight to the emergency room.

Anaphylactic symptoms are:
- breathing problems
- severe swelling of the face, lips, and throat
- increased heart rate/racing pulse
- sweating
- fainting
- ultimately death if not treated quickly

A food intolerance is not life threatening but can be highly unpleasant. Symptoms are usually associated with the stomach, such as vomiting and diarrhea, stomach cramps, or a headache or rash.

foods that can cause food allergies

There are eight food substances that cause most food allergies. Even the tiniest exposure to a specific food can cause children and adults who are allergic to suffer reactions, whether they have consumed it themselves or not. It even could be that someone is eating peanuts when someone with a peanut allergy walks into the same room. The eight foods are:

- dairy
- eggs
- peanuts
- shellfish
- gluten (usually from wheat)
- tree nuts (such as cashews, walnuts, pecans)
- soy
- fish

dairy products

Dairy products are made from cow's milk and include yogurt, cheese, cream, crème fraîche, and butter. Babies under 6 months old should not be given any dairy products. Cow's milk should not be used as a drink for babies until they are at least 12 months old, nor should cow's milk itself be used in cooking for babies under 12 months.

Cow's milk hinders iron absorption. Iron is critical to support the growth of a human baby. Also, cow's milk can be difficult for babies to digest. Other dairy products such as yogurt and cheese are cultured and are easier on young digestive systems. This is why it is fine to give babies 6 months and older dairy products, but not cow's milk until they are 12 months. Do not give babies or toddlers unpasteurized cheese, milk, or other dairy products, goat or sheep's cheese, or mold-ripened cheese, because of the risk of listeria.

gluten & wheat

Gluten is a protein found in wheat and other grains, such as barley, and can be a cause of allergy and intolerance. Oats do not contain gluten, but may be contaminated with it during the manufacturing process, so to be cautious you should introduce oats no earlier than 6 months old, and if there is no adverse reaction, you can move on to wheat. Wheat is a common cause of allergy and intolerance, so introduce to your baby after 9 months old. Wheat or gluten intolerance (celiac disease) is often a lifelong condition that will mean total restriction of consuming anything with wheat or gluten. Please consult your pediatrician about this issue.

eggs

Eggs are a good source of protein and iron; however, they must be thoroughly cooked. Eggs can be a source of salmonella, a source of food poisoning. Avoid foods using unpasteurized raw egg, such as homemade mayonnaise, mousses, and ice cream, and do not allow your baby to lick the spoon if you have been making cake batter. Commercial mayonnaise and ice creams are generally pasteurized, but always check the label before offering to a young child. When your baby is 6 months or older, you can introduce eggs in a small amount, as some babies are highly allergic to eggs. (This is uncommon, but it's best to be safe.)

soy

Soy is a legume, part of the pea and bean family, as are peanuts. (If children and adults are allergic to soybeans and soy products, they might be able to eat other legumes with no reaction.) Avoid edamame beans, soy sauce, miso, soybeans, tofu, textured vegetable protein (TVP), tamari, and tempeh. Soy protein is a common food additive that can be included in soups, stock, gum, starches, medicines, flavorings, and colorings, so read the labels carefully.

peanuts

Peanut allergy is becoming more common, and many children and adults who are allergic to peanuts and peanut oil are also allergic to tree nuts. People with severe nut allergies may react to only very small, or trace, amounts of nuts.

tree nuts

These are nuts that grow on trees, such as cashews, pecans, walnuts, and almonds. Pine nuts also fall into this category, although they are not strictly a nut but a seed. If your child is allergic to peanuts, it is highly likely that they may also be allergic to tree nuts. Allergy to cashews may be linked to bad reactions to poison ivy, so if you or your child has reacted badly to poison ivy, be wary of cashews. Be careful when buying pesto, in case nuts other than pine nuts have been included, and also read the labels of body lotion, shampoo, suntan lotion, and other cosmetics, as tree nut oil is frequently used as an ingredient. They do not have to be ingested to cause a reaction; just touching an allergen can start a reaction for someone who is severely allergic.

fish & shellfish

Start your baby on white fish such as flounder beginning at 6 months, and move them on to salmon and other oily fish if they show no reaction to the white fish. But do not give babies or toddlers swordfish, marlin, shark, tilefish, or orange roughy, because these carry a high risk of mercury in their flesh. Also be very cautious of mackerel, tuna, grouper, bluefish, and Chilean sea bass because they contain some mercury. Give them only in moderation. Providing there is no history of shellfish allergy in your family, shellfish should be fine to introduce to babies over 12 months old. Just be sure that the shellfish is from a reliable source and is well cooked.

other foods to restrict

The following foods may cause an adverse reaction with your baby, so introduce gradually, and monitor your baby carefully. With any adverse reaction, reintroduce after 12 months.

citrus & other acidic fruit

Tomatoes, kiwifruit, and pineapples can be acidic, so introduce gradually after 6 months and watch your baby's reaction carefully. Some babies love them and have no problems, others have an adverse reaction which means you should hold off and reintroduce after 12 months. Citrus fruit tends to be acidic and can possibly lead to an upset tummy in young babies. It's best to introduce any citrus (including oranges, lemons, limes, grapefruit, and clementines) gradually after 9 months, and montor their reaction.

strawberries & other berries

Strawberries are a common allergen, so it is advisable not to introduce them until baby is over 12 months old. Raspberries and blackberries are slightly acidic and can cause an upset tummy, so it may be suitable to wait until your baby is 12 months old.

honey, maple syrup & corn syrup

Never give a baby under 12 months old honey, maple syrup, or corn syrup. These products may contain the bacteria *Clostridium botulinum*, which produces toxins in a baby's intestines leading to infant botulism. Once babies are over a year old, their intestines have matured sufficiently to prevent this bacteria from growing.

sugary foods

Do not feed your baby sugary foods, such as cakes, cookies, and chocolate, before 12 months. Babies do not need these foods, and the longer they are kept away from them the more likely they will try — and like — fresh fruit and vegetables and other healthy options.

salt

We add salt to our food to make it taste better, but babies will accept food for how it tastes without salt (as we adults would if we had never tried it). Salt is dangerous to babies. It can lead to high blood pressure and possible kidney failure.

equipment for making baby food

There's nothing specific that you must have for making baby food, but the following items — which are common in most kitchens — are very helpful.

digital weighing scales, measuring cups & spoons
These make your life easy by ensuring that the quantities are correct, especially when baking muffins and bread. Small measuring cups are especially helpful for making the small quantities needed for babies.

blenders & food processors
When you're pureeing a small amount of food, a handheld immersion blender is your best bet. They also are useful to puree soups right in the pan. Blenders and food processors are good for bigger quantities such as for making smoothies, and they can be used to make bread crumbs, puree hummus, and prepare other dips.

potato masher, potato ricer & food mill
A handheld potato masher will make quick work of mashing a pan of boiled potatoes, as well as any cooked root vegtables or stewed fruits. Potato ricers give a much finer and smoother texture and also are good for preparing baby food. A food mill is a stainless steel utensil that grinds meat, poultry, fish, vegetables, and fruit to a puree.

standing mixers & mixing bowls

Heavy-duty electric mixers make short work of mixing pizza and bread dough, pancakes and muffins, and beating eggs. Some models come with a wide range of attachments to help you make your own pasta dough and ground meat. Lightweight stainless steel bowls that are dishwasher-proof and unbreakable are a sound investment, especially when your toddler starts to help you cook.

chopping boards

Keep one chopping board purely for raw meat to prevent cross contamination and make sure that it is washed thoroughly after use. A second chopping board can be used for fruits and vegetables, cooked meats, and other items you need to chop. A nonstick plastic board suitable for dishwashers is ideal. Avoid glass chopping boards, as they will blunt your knives and tend to be slippery to work with.

stovetop cookware & ovenware

Solid stainless steel saucepans in different sizes are invaluable. A steamer basket (which you set over a pan of boiling water) is good for cooking vegetables, because they are more nutritious steamed than boiled. A nonstick skillet is good for reducing the amount of oil and fat you cook with, making food healthier for baby and the rest of the family. Baking pans and muffin tins should be nonstick. Look for good-quality, solid pans. It is worth paying a little more, knowing that they will last you a long time.

parchment paper & plastic wrap
Use parchment paper to line baking pans and to roll pastry, cookie dough, and bread on. You will not need to use as much flour on the work surface, so there is much less cleaning to do. Plastic wrap is essential to cover food to be kept in the refrigerator.

timers
When you have a baby or toddler, you will need a kitchen timer to remind you of foods you have cooking. It is difficult to remember everything when you are distracted by children.

ice cube trays, freezer containers & bags
When starting to make baby food, you'll find ice cube trays are ideal for freezing purees. Each cube is a one-ounce serving. The recipes in this book provide more than one serving, so you can freeze cubes for meals for the next few weeks, or you could even enlist the help of family or friends to help you out in the first few months of life with a baby! After the cubes are frozen, transfer them to a freezer-weight plastic bag, label the bag with the name of the food and the date, and replace in the freezer.

As your baby grows, you will need bigger containers. Freezer containers with lids come in different sizes and are ideal for freezing individual meal portions. Always label the container with the name of the food and the date it was made, and use the oldest food first.

baby food safety techniques

Food safety and personal hygiene must be especially stringent when preparing baby food.

- Do not handle food with unwashed hands, and wash your hands thoroughly after handling raw meat, poultry, and fish. Keep utensils and boards very clean.

- Freshly cooked food must be cooled quickly, within 90 minutes, and then placed in a sealed container in the refrigerator. If it is to be frozen, transfer the freshly made food to an ice cube tray (if making one-ounce servings) or single-serving freezer containers with lids, and cool quickly before placing in the freezer. To cool food quickly, place the ice cube tray or freezer container in an ice bath or cold water in the sink.

- Be sure that raw meat and fish are stored at the bottom of the refrigerator or freezer to avoid cross-contamination with ready-to-eat food.

- Never put hot or warm food in the refrigerator or freezer, because the food will raise the temperature of the rest of the food inside. This could lead to bacteria breeding, which could lead to food poisoning.

- Thoroughly defrost food before reheating, and only reheat once. The safest way to defrost is in the refrigerator overnight, or in the microwave. Do not defrost food under hot water or by leaving it on the counter, because bacteria will be able to multiply to unsafe levels.

- When feeding your baby, transfer the food in small amounts to a dish so you can add more with a clean spoon if baby is enjoying it. Do not feed your baby directly out of the container, because the spoon baby has eaten from could contaminate the food in the container.

- You can use your microwave for cooking and reheating: please follow the manufacturer's instructions. Microwave instructions are not included within the recipes due to varying power settings. If you are using a microwave, always ensure food is piping hot before serving.

- Always, always have a responsible adult supervise your baby's mealtimes and snacktimes.

baby's first foods

It's an exciting time when your baby is ready to

start eating solid foods. All foods should be pureed

and have a sloppy, liquid consistency. If needed,

add breast milk, formula, or the cooking liquid to

the puree to achieve this very thin consistency.

Have fun with it!

baby porridge

see variations page 43

Porridge for infants is made by grinding uncooked rice, never oats. Oats should not be given to babies before they are 6 months old, because oats may contain a small amount of gluten, a potential allergen.

3 cups brown rice
scant 1 cup water
breast milk or infant formula

Grind the rice in a blender, food processor, or clean coffee/spice grinder until it becomes a very, very fine powder. Store in an airtight container and keep in a cool dry place for up to 3 months.

To cook one portion, place 1 cup water in a small pan and bring to a boil. Add 1/4 cup ground rice powder and simmer, stirring constantly, for 10 minutes. Remove from the heat and stir in enough breast milk or formula to achieve the desired consistency. Cool quickly and refrigerate within 30 minutes if you wish to keep some for another meal.

Use within 24 hours. Cooled porridge can be frozen immediately. Place in a freezerproof container, label, and freeze for up to 1 month. To use from frozen, defrost thoroughly and heat through fully, then serve.

Makes 8–12 portions

melon puree

see variations page 44

Ripe melon — cantaloupe, Galia, or honeydew — is easy to mash for babies. It has a mild flavor and complements other fruit well. Melon is high in water content, so you may not need extra liquid when it is pureed.

1 whole melon
10–14 fl. oz. breast milk or formula

Slice and peel the melon, and chop the flesh into chunks. Mash with a fork or puree in a blender or food processor, adding breast milk or formula until it is a semi-liquid consistency. Serve 3–4 tablespoons per portion for young babies.

You can either cover and refrigerate for up to 48 hours, or freeze in ice cube trays until solid, then transfer to a freezer bag, label, and use within 1 month. To defrost, simply remove 2 or 3 cubes of frozen melon puree and let come to room temperature, stir, and serve.

Makes 20–24 portions

apple puree

see variations page 45

Apples such as Braeburn, Gala, Golden Delicious, and Fuji work well in this recipe.

8 apples
5–8 fl. oz. breast milk or formula

Peel, core, and chop or slice the apples. Place the apple pieces in a saucepan with enough water to just cover them, then boil or steam until the apple pieces are tender. Drain (and reserve) any excess water, then mash or puree the apples with a little breast milk, formula, or the cooking water until the puree has the required consistency.

You can cover and refrigerate the pureed apple for 24 hours. Alternatively, freeze in ice cube trays until solid, then transfer to a freezer bag, label, and use within 1 month. To defrost, simply remove 2 or 3 cubes of frozen apple puree and let come to room temperature, stir, and serve.

Makes 30 portions

banana puree

see variations page 46

Bananas are almost the perfect food. Fresh, they are easily carried in a bag, giving you an instant baby meal. All you need is a fork to mash the banana with. Choose ripe bananas, as they are easier to mash than unripe bananas. Also, babies can have difficulty digesting unripe bananas.

4 ripe bananas, peeled
3–4 tbsp. breast milk or formula

Mash or puree the flesh of the bananas with a little breast milk or formula until it has the desired consistency.

You can refrigerate the mashed banana for 24 hours, but it tends to go brown quickly. Freeze mashed bananas in ice cube trays until solid, then transfer to a freezer bag, label, and use within 1 month. To defrost, simply remove 2 or 3 cubes of frozen banana puree and let come to room temperature, stir, and serve.

Makes 4–8 portions

mashed sweet potato

see variations page 47

Sweet potatoes and yams mash easily, are easy to digest, are naturally sweet, and make an ideal first food for babies. You can bake or steam the potato.

2 sweet potatoes
2–4 tbsp. breast milk or formula

To bake: Preheat the oven to 425°F. Wash the sweet potatoes and prick all over with a fork to prevent it from bursting while it is cooking. Wrap the potates in aluminum foil and place onto a small baking pan to stop any sticky juices from dripping into the oven. Bake for 30–60 minutes until soft. Remove from the oven, discard the foil, and let cool. Slit the potatoes lengthwise, scoop out the flesh, and discard the skin.

To steam: Wash and peel the potatoes and chop into cubes. Place the potato cubes in a colander set over a pan of boiling water, cover with a lid, and steam for 10–15 minutes until tender.

Mash or puree the baked or steamed potato flesh with a little breast milk or formula.

You can either cover and refrigerate for up to 48 hours, or freeze in ice cube trays until solid, then transfer to a freezer bag, label, and use within 1 month. To defrost, simply remove 2 or 3 cubes of frozen mashed sweet potato and let come to room temperature, stir, heat through fully, and serve.

Makes 10–12 portions

mashed potato

see variations page 48

Potatoes are high in fiber and a great vegetable to introduce to babies early in their weaning. By adding brightly colored vegetables to the potato, you introduce different flavors and textures, and suddenly a plain old potato becomes much more exciting. Always introduce new foods one at a time, a few days apart.

2 potatoes

To bake: Preheat the oven to 425°F. Wash the potatoes and prick all over with a fork to prevent from bursting while cooking. Wrap the potatoes in aluminum foil and place onto the top shelf of your oven. Bake for 50–60 minutes, until soft. Remove from the oven, discard the foil, and let cool. Slit the potatoes lengthwise, scoop out the flesh, and discard the skins.

To steam: Wash and peel the potatoes, chop into cubes, and steam over boiling water for 20–25 minutes, until the cubes are tender. To boil: Wash and peel the potatoes and chop into cubes. Bring a pan of water to a boil, add the potatoes, and simmer for 15–20 minutes, until the cubes are soft. Mash or puree the cooked potatoes with a little breast milk or formula, and serve.

You can either cover and refrigerate for up to 48 hours, or freeze in ice cube trays until solid, then transfer to a freezer bag, label, and use within 1 month. To defrost, simply remove 2 or 3 cubes of frozen mashed potato and let come to room temperature, stir, heat through fully, and serve.

Makes 10–12 portions

mashed butternut squash

see variations page 49

Butternut squash freezes really well. A whole squash will fill up a whole ice cube tray and give you extra to make a family meal. It is a very versatile vegetable, and delicious roasted.

1 small butternut squash
1 tbsp. mild olive oil

To roast: Preheat the oven to 425°F. Halve the butternut squash and scoop out the seeds. Cut the halves into slices, brush with a little olive oil, and roast for 20–30 minutes, until soft. Remove it from the oven, set aside to cool slightly, and then peel. Puree or mash with a little breast milk or formula.

To steam: Halve the butternut squash, scoop out the seeds, then peel and chop in 3/4-inch cubes. Steam over boiling water for 15–20 minutes until tender. Mash or puree the flesh with a little breast milk or formula, and serve. Leave the breast milk out of the portions for the whole family.

You can either cover and refrigerate for up to 48 hours, or freeze in ice cube trays until solid, then transfer to a freezer bag, label, and use within 1 month. To defrost, simply remove 2 or 3 cubes of frozen mashed butternut squash and let come to room temperature, stir, heat through fully, and serve.

Makes 8–10 portions

rutabaga & apple puree

see variations page 50

Rutabaga has a strong flavor, which makes it a good first food because it introduces babies to strong flavors from an early age. Adding some apple, however, helps to tone down the strong flavor as well as adding a little sweetness. This puree freezes really well.

1 small rutabaga
2 apples

Wash, peel, and chop the rutabaga. Place in a steamer over boiling water and cook for 10–15 minutes, until partially tender.

Peel, core, and chop or slice the apples. Add them to the steamer. Steam the rutabaga and apple for about 10 minutes, until tender. Puree or mash with breast milk or formula.

You can either cover and refrigerate for up to 48 hours, or freeze in ice cube trays until solid, then transfer to a freezer bag, label, and use within 1 month. To defrost, simply remove 2 or 3 cubes of frozen rutabaga and apple puree and let come to room temperature, stir, and serve.

Makes 8–10 portions

papaya rice pudding

see variations page 51

Ripe papaya is easy to prepare and mash because of its high water content. Adding pureed brown rice to papaya makes a delicious fruity meal, a little like a baby version of a baked rice pudding. You could make rice pudding for the rest of the family and serve it with fresh papaya so the whole family would be eating the same pudding.

1/2 cup uncooked brown rice
1 cup water
1 ripe papaya

Place the rice and water in a saucepan, bring to a boil, cover, and simmer for 20 minutes, or until the liquid has been absorbed and the rice is cooked. Puree with a little breast milk or formula until you reach a thick soupy consistency.

Halve the papaya, then scoop out and discard the black seeds. Scoop out the orange flesh and mash or puree.

Combine the cooked rice puree and papaya, adding a little more breast milk or formula as needed. Serve.

Make sure the rice is cooled for no more than 30 minutes at room temperature before placing in the refrigerator, and use within 24 hours. Cooled rice can be frozen immediately. Place in a freezerproof container, label, and freeze for up to 1 month. To use from frozen, defrost thoroughly and heat through fully, then serve.

Makes 6–8 portions

variations

baby porridge

see base recipe page 27

banana baby porridge
Prepare the basic recipe, then add 1 teaspoon mashed banana. You may need to add more liquid.

apple baby porridge
Prepare the basic recipe, then stir in 1 teaspoon apple puree (page 30).

blueberry baby porridge
Prepare the basic recipe. Mash and strain 1 tablespoon fresh blueberries, then stir into the porridge.

fruity baby porridge
Prepare the basic recipe, then stir in a teaspoonful of a mixture of mashed banana and strained blueberries and a little more liquid if necessary.

baby porridge with apricots
Prepare the basic recipe. Meanwhile, cook 2–3 dried apricots in a little water until tender, puree, and stir a teaspoonful into the porridge. Refrigerate or freeze the remaining apricot puree.

variations

melon puree

see base recipe page 29

melonocado
Mash 1/2 avocado with a slice of melon, adding a little breast milk or formula to achieve the required consistency.

melon & banana puree
Mash 1 banana with a slice of melon for a slightly thicker puree, and thin it down with a little breast milk or formula if required.

melon & apple puree
Prepare the basic recipe, adding 1 tablespoon apple puree (page 30).

melon & pear with cinnamon puree
Prepare the basic recipe, adding 1 tablespoon pureed fresh pear and a pinch of ground cinnamon.

melon & blueberry puree
Mash 1/2 cup fresh or thawed frozen blueberries, and press through a fine-mesh strainer to remove any seeds. Add to the melon, puree and serve as before.

variations

apple puree

see base recipe page 30

apple & cinnamon puree
Prepare the basic recipe, adding 2 teaspoons ground cinnamon when cooking
the apple.

purple puree
Prepare the basic recipe, but when the apple is almost cooked, add 1/2 cup
fresh or thawed frozen blueberries and continue cooking for 5 minutes
before pureeing.

apple & pear puree
Prepare the basic recipe, adding 4 peeled, cored, and chopped or sliced pears to
the saucepan to cook with the apple.

mango & apple puree
Prepare the basic recipe. Puree 1 fresh mango. Stir into the apple puree.

apple & banana puree
Prepare the basic recipe, adding 1 mashed banana to the saucepan to cook with
the apple.

variations

banana puree

see base recipe page 32

bananacado
Mash 2 ripe avocados with the banana, adding a little breast milk or formula to achieve the required consistency.

blue banana
Prepare the basic recipe. Lightly cook 4 tablespoons fresh blueberries in a little water for 5 minutes, until they collapse. Puree and press through a sieve, then stir into the mashed banana.

banapple
Instead of the basic recipe, add a little freshly squeezed apple juice to the banana instead of breast milk or formula.

peachy banana
Instead of the basic recipe, peel, pit, and puree 2 ripe peaches. Add to the banana along with a little freshly squeezed apple juice to achieve the required consistency.

variations

mashed sweet potato

see base recipe page 34

sweet potato & leek
Prepare the basic recipe, using the steaming method. Add 2 chopped leeks
(white part only) to the colander with the sweet potato. Puree with breast
milk or formula.

green & orange swirly supper
Cook the sweet potatoes using the steaming method. Add 2 cups fresh baby
spinach to the colander for the final 10 minutes of cooking time. Cook until
tender. Puree the spinach and the sweet potato with breast milk or formula.

sweet potato & zucchini
Prepare the basic recipe, using the steaming method, and adding 2 zucchini,
washed and chopped, to the colander with the sweet potatoes.

sweet potato & green beans
Prepare the basic recipe, using the steaming method, Add 2 ounces fresh or
frozen green beans to the colander for the final 10 minutes of cooking.

sweet potato & carrot
Prepare the basic recipe, using the steaming method, and adding 2 peeled
and chopped carrots to the colander with the sweet potatoes.

variations

mashed potato

see base recipe page 36

orange mash
Prepare the basic recipe. Wash, peel, and chop 2 medium carrots, then steam or boil for 10–15 minutes, until tender. Mash or puree, and add to the mashed potato.

yellow mash
Prepare the basic recipe. Wash, peel, and chop 1 yellow rutabaga then steam or boil for 20–25 minutes, until tender. Mash or puree, and add to the mashed potato.

green mash
Cook the potatoes. Steam 2 cups fresh baby spinach leaves for 10 minutes, until tender, then puree with the potato, and a little breast milk or formula.

pink mash
Prepare the basic recipe. Wash, peel, and chop 2 fresh beets. Steam or boil for 20–25 minutes, until tender, then mash or puree, and add to the mashed potato.

variations

mashed butternut squash

see base recipe page 39

butternut squash & sweet potato mash
Prepare the basic recipe, adding 1 washed, peeled, and chopped sweet potato to the steamer with the butternut squash.

butternut squash & carrot mash
Prepare the basic recipe, adding 1 washed, peeled, and chopped medium carrot to the steamer with the butternut squash.

popeye's squash
Prepare the basic recipe, adding 1 cup fresh baby spinach to the steamer for the last 10 minutes of cooking time. Add a pinch of ground nutmeg when mashing or pureeing the vegetables.

squash & apple porridge
Prepare the basic recipe. Then stir in 1 tablespoon apple puree (page 30) and 1 tablespoon baby porridge (page 27).

butternut squash & cauliflower mash
Prepare the basic recipe, adding 5–6 washed cauliflower florets to the steamer with the butternut squash.

variations

rutabaga & apple puree

see base recipe page 40

rutabaga, apple & carrot puree
Prepare the basic recipe, adding 1 washed, peeled, and chopped medium carrot to the steamer with the rutabaga.

rutabaga & sweet potato mash
Prepare the basic recipe, replacing the apples with 1 washed, peeled, and chopped sweet potato. Add it to the steamer with the rutabaga.

rutabaga, apple & pumpkin mash
Prepare the basic recipe, adding the cubes from 1 peeled slice of pumpkin to the steamer with the rutabaga.

rutabaga, apple & parsnip mash
Prepare the basic recipe, adding 1 washed, peeled, and chopped parsnip to the steamer with the rutabaga.

variations

papaya rice pudding

see base recipe page 42

melon & papaya rice pudding
Prepare the basic recipe. Puree a slice of ripe cantaloupe or Galia melon and stir it into the pudding. Add a little breast milk or formula if necessary to achieve the required consistency.

peachy rice pudding
Prepare the basic recipe, but replace the papaya with 1 washed, peeled, and pitted ripe peach.

apricot & papaya rice pudding
Prepare the basic recipe. Lightly cook 2–3 dried apricots in a little water for 5 minutes, until they soften. Puree, press through a sieve, and stir into the papaya rice pudding.

apple & papaya rice pudding
Prepare the basic recipe. Peel, core, and slice 1 apple. Cook it in a little water until tender, then puree and stir into the papaya rice pudding.

tropical fruit pudding
Prepare the basic recipe. Wash and pit 1 ripe mango. Mash or puree, then stir into the papaya rice pudding.

moving on:
6–9 months

Your baby can now eat virtually the same food as

the rest of the family, with no added salt. Make sure

you check that all ingredients are recommended for

the age of your baby. Your baby will grow up

knowing that everyone eats together.

banana yogurt

see variations page 89

Once your baby is 6 months old, you can offer yogurt for breakfast. Plain full-fat yogurt is the best option. Sweeten and flavor it by adding pureed fresh fruit.

3 ripe bananas, peeled
6 tbsp. plain full-fat yogurt

Mash or puree the flesh of the banana with the yogurt. As baby grows, leave the fruit with more lumps.

You can cover and refrigerate the banana yogurt for 24 hours, but it tends to go brown quickly. Freeze banana yogurt in ice cube trays until solid, then transfer to a freezer bag, label, and use within 1 month. To defrost, simply remove 2 or 3 cubes of frozen banana yogurt and let come to room temperature, stir, and serve.

Makes 10–12 portions

scrambled eggs

see variations page 90

This is an easy introduction to eggs for babies over 6 months, which can be shared with the whole family. For babies close to 1 year, serve with toast fingers.

1 tsp. butter
1–2 eggs, beaten

1 tbsp. milk (use breast milk or formula for
babies under 12 months)

Melt the butter in a small saucepan or skillet.

Beat the eggs with the milk. Once the butter has melted, tip in the eggs and stir constantly with a wooden spoon until thoroughly cooked.

Makes 1–2 portions

oat porridge

see variations page 91

Probably one of the easiest and most delicious breakfasts on the planet. After your baby is 6 months old, you can introduce oats to his diet. As with any new foods, when giving oats for the first time, monitor your baby's reaction to the food to check for any allergies. It is possible to double up on quantities and refrigerate or freeze, but it is just as quick to make fresh for each serving.

4 tbsp. quick-cooking rolled oats
1 cup milk (use breast milk or formula
for babies under 12 months)

Put the oats and milk in a saucepan. Slowly bring to a boil, stirring continuously. Simmer for 5–6 minutes, until the oats are soft and the mixture is thick. Remove from heat. Add a little extra cold breast milk or formula to cool and thin the porridge, if desired.

If you prefer, cook the porridge in a microwave. Heat on high for 1 minute, stir, and heat on high for another minute, stir, and add cold breast milk or formula if desired. Serve immediately.

Porridge should be eaten immediately, or cool at room temperature for no more than 1 hour, and freeze porridge in ice cube trays until solid. Transfer to a freezer bag, label, and use within 1 month. To defrost, simply remove 2 or 3 cubes of frozen porridge and let come to room temperature, stir, heat through fully, and serve.

Makes 4–8 portions

baby omelet

see variations page 92

An omelet cooked this way — flat, like a pancake — is fabulous as a finger food, so it's suitable for baby-led weaning, if desired.

1 tsp. butter or a little olive oil
2 eggs, beaten

In a small skillet set over medium heat, melt the butter or heat the olive oil. Pour in the eggs and shake, so the eggs cover the bottom of the pan. Leave the pan on the burner and let the eggs set. Then, flip the omelet over, a little like a pancake, to thoroughly cook the other side.

Fold omelet over and cut into very small strips for baby, to serve.

Freeze extra portions in freezerproof containers, label, and use within 1 month. To defrost, simply remove from the freezer and let come to room temperature, heat through fully, and serve.

Makes 2–4 portions

french toast

see variations page 93

This is a true taste of childhood for many of us, which still tastes great to adults. But adults like their French toast (a.k.a. eggy bread) with butter, maple syrup, and bacon. Babies under 1 year should not be given syrup or bacon, but they won't know what they're missing. They don't even need butter to enjoy their eggy bread, but it is good served with a couple of spoonfuls of apple puree (see recipe page 30).

6 eggs
6 tbsp. milk (use breast milk or formula for under 12 months)

6 thick slice bread (crusts removed for younger ages)
a little butter

Beat the eggs with the milk. Pour mixture into a shallow, wide bowl or deep plate. Dunk each slice of bread into the egg mixture until it's totally coated. Repeat until all bread is coated in egg.

Heat the butter in a nonstick frying pan. Fry the bread until golden, turn over, and repeat with the other side. Remove from the pan and cut into fingers. One slice of bread will be sufficient for younger babies.

Place uncooked extra portions in a single layer on a greased cookie sheet and put in the freezer. When frozen, transfer to freezer bags, label, and use within 1 month. To use from frozen, simply place the frozen french toast on a baking sheet and bake at 425°F for 8 minutes, then turn and bake for an additional 10–12 minutes.

Makes 6 servings

spring vegetable soup

see variations page 94

As the name suggests, this soup is made with spring vegetables in season. It should be light and fresh-tasting. If you are making this for the whole family, double the quantities (for a family of 4–5).

2 medium carrots
2 leeks, white part only
1/2 head savoy cabbage

1 tsp. butter or a little olive oil
4 1/2 cups low-sodium vegetable or
    chicken stock

Wash, peel, and chop the carrots, leeks, and cabbage. In a pan set over low heat, melt the butter or heat the olive oil. Add the vegetables and sauté for 5 minutes. Add the stock and bring to a boil. Cover the pan and simmer for 20–25 minutes, until the carrot is soft. Puree for babies up to 12 months.

Freeze extra portions in freezerproof containers, label, and use within 3 months.
To use from frozen, carefully defrost. Heat through fully before serving.

Makes 12–16 portions

leek & potato soup

see variations page 95

This is a lovely warming soup. The potatoes make it thick and easier for a baby to eat. If you are making this for the whole family, double the quantities (for a family of 4–5).

1 potato
1 leek

1 tsp. butter or a little olive oil
2 cups low-sodium vegetable or chicken stock

Wash, peel, and chop the potato and leek (white portion only).

In a large pan, melt the butter or heat the olive oil. Add the potatoes and leeks and sauté for 5 minutes over low heat.

Add the stock and bring to a boil. Cover and simmer for 30 minutes, until the potato is soft. Puree the mixture. Serve warm.

Freeze extra portions in freezerproof containers, label, and use within 3 months. To use from frozen, carefully defrost. Heat through fully before serving.

Makes 6–8 portions

chicken soup

see variations page 96

There are lots of stories about chicken soup being healing, and good for you if you have a cold. Chicken soup is definitely warming, and is very nutritious. Puree this soup for babies up to the age of 12 months; thereafter, make sure the chicken is chopped in very small pieces until your child is over 3 years old to prevent choking.

2 chicken portions (breast or leg)
2 carrots
2 small onions

2 stalks celery
4 cups low-sodium chicken stock

Skin and chop the chicken. If the chicken is on the bone, then you can skin it and put it in whole. Finely chop the carrots, onions, and celery. Add all the ingredients to the stock and bring to a boil. Cover and simmer for 30–40 minutes, until the vegetables are tender and the chicken is cooked.

Puree the soup and serve warm. If you used chicken on the bone, shred the meat from the bone and put it back in the soup before pureeing.

Freeze extra portions in small freezerproof containers, label, and use within 1 month. To use from frozen, carefully defrost. Heat through fully before serving.

Makes 8–12 portions

classic tomato sauce

see variations page 97

A very versatile sauce full of antioxidants and vitamins from the tomatoes. Serve with cooked pasta, rice, or use as a dip or pizza sauce (see page 211). Babies occasionally have an adverse reaction to tomatoes at this early stage, although others love them. Observe your baby carefully, and if there is any kind of allergic response, wait until after 12 months to reintroduce tomatoes.

2 tbsp. olive oil
2 red or white onions, finely chopped
2 cloves garlic, finely chopped
16 ripe plum tomatoes, skinned and chopped,
    or 2 (14-oz.) cans whole plum tomatoes

2 cups water
large handful of fresh basil leaves, washed
    and torn

Heat the oil in a skillet or saucepan with a lid and gently sauté the onion over low to medium heat for 10–15 minutes, until it is translucent and soft.

Stir in the tomatoes and water. Bring to a boil, cover with the lid, reduce to a simmer, and cook for 20 minutes. Remove the lid, stir in the basil leaves, and simmer for 5 minutes more, uncovered. Puree mixture in a blender or food processor.

Let sauce cool, then use or store in the refrigerator for up to 3 days, or freeze immediately and use within 1 month. To use from frozen, carefully defrost. Heat through fully before serving.

Makes 8–12 portions

mediterranean roasted vegetables

see variations page 98

This sauce is packed full of goodness, with its special selection of different-colored vegetables to get the best mix of vitamins and minerals. This is a great sauce for all the family, and ideal to pour over cooked pasta.

1 red or white onion, roughly chopped
1 small eggplant, roughly chopped
1 small zucchini, roughly chopped
1 sweet red pepper, roughly chopped
1 sweet orange pepper, roughly chopped

1 sweet yellow or green pepper, chopped
1 tbsp. olive oil
1 clove garlic, finely chopped
1 (15-oz.) can whole tomatoes
1 3/4 cups low-sodium vegetable stock

Preheat the oven to 400°F. Place chopped vegetables on a baking pan, drizzle with the olive oil, and sprinkle with the garlic. Roast for 20–25 minutes, turning them over halfway, until the vegetables are soft and slightly brown at the edges. Check the vegetables occasionally throughout the cooking time to make sure they don't burn. Transfer to a saucepan and add the tomatoes and vegetable stock. Bring to a boil, cover the pan, and simmer for 20 minutes.

Puree in a food processor. If the sauce seems thin, reduce it slightly by boiling rapidly for 5 minutes, until it is thickened. For older babies (12 months +), and other members of the family, allow the sauce to have more lumps and serve with pasta or couscous, or in baked potatoes.

Store in the refrigerator for up to 3 days, or freeze immediately and use within 1 month. To use from frozen, carefully defrost. Heat through fully before serving.

Makes 6–8 child portions or 3–4 adult portions

carrot & chicken dinner

see variations page 99

Chicken is mild in flavor and a good form of protein to start your baby on. When it is pureed, however, it can be quite thick, so it will need a lot of liquid to thin it to a consistency easy for your baby to swallow. Adding root vegetables such as carrots helps make the chicken more palatable. If your baby is low in iron, replace the chicken breast with thigh meat, which is higher in iron.

2 skinless and boneless chicken breasts
2 carrots, washed, peeled, and chopped

breast milk or formula, as needed

Poaching is an ideal way of cooking chicken, because the chicken stays moist, is easy to puree, and retains most of its nutrients. Preheat the oven to 375°F. Place the chicken in a baking dish with 1/2 inch of boiling water. Add the chopped carrot, making sure it is covered with water, and cover the dish with aluminum foil. Cook for 20–30 minutes, or until the chicken is cooked through. Do not let it overcook, or it will be tough. Remove the chicken and carrot from the liquid, and puree with breast milk or formula, or some of the cooking liquid, to the desired consistency. If you want to steam the chicken, place it and the chopped carrot in a steamer over boiling water. Steam for 20–30 minutes, until the chicken is cooked through. Puree with a little breast milk or formula.

Store in the refrigerator for up to 2 days, or freeze immediately and use within 1 month. To use from frozen, carefully defrost. Heat through fully before serving.

Makes 8–10 child portions

turkey casserole

see variations page 100

This classic casserole includes lots of vegetables. It is a great meal for the whole family and easily adjusted for young babies.

1 tbsp. sunflower oil
1 onion
2 carrots

1 lb. thinly sliced turkey breast cutlets
1 tsp. chopped fresh thyme
1 cup low-sodium chicken stock

Preheat the oven to 350°F. Heat the oil in a nonstick skillet. Peel and finely chop the onion and carrots. Brown the turkey in the oil, turning often until all sides are colored. Transfer to a heavy casserole and add the remaining ingredients. Bring to a boil, then cover with a lid, transfer to the oven, and cook for 40–45 minutes, until the turkey is cooked through.

Remove from the oven, puree for babies under 9 months, or cut up the turkey pieces for babies under 12 months. Serve with mashed potato or rice (pureed for babies).

Store in the refrigerator for up to 2 days, or freeze immediately and use within 1 month. To use from frozen, carefully defrost. Heat through fully before serving.

Makes 6–8 child portions or 2 adult portions

beef goulash

see variations page 101

This Hungarian dish combines inexpensive cuts of beef with potatoes for a hearty warming stew. Goulash is even better eaten the day after it is made, because the potatoes break down, thickening the stew, and the flavors are absorbed, leaving a thick, comforting dish. If you want, you can make this goulash in a slow cooker.

1 onion
1 tbsp. sunflower oil
3 fresh tomatoes or 1 (8-oz.) can chopped
    tomatoes
1/2 small red bell pepper

1 tsp. mild paprika
10 1/2 oz. lean steak for braising, finely sliced
1 cup low-sodium beef stock
1/2 lb. potatoes, peeled and chopped

Peel and finely chop the onion. Heat the oil in a nonstick skillet and fry the onion over low to medium heat for 10 minutes, until soft and translucent. Transfer to a baking dish with a lid that can be used on the stovetop. Peel, seed, and chop the fresh tomatoes and add to the dish. (If using the canned tomatoes, just pour in the tomatoes and their juices.) Finely chop the pepper and add to the baking dish along with the paprika. Cook for 3–4 minutes over low to medium heat. Add the steak slices to the dish, cook for 2–3 minutes, then add the stock. Bring to a boil, and reduce to a simmer. Add the potatoes to the pan. Put on the lid, and cook for 2 hours on the stovetop or in the oven at 325°F. Allow to cool a little, then puree before serving.

Store in the refrigerator for up to 2 days, or freeze immediately and use within 1 month. To use from frozen, carefully defrost. Heat through fully before serving.

Makes 8–10 child portions or 2 adult portions

chicken curry & rice

see variations page 102

This is a basic chicken curry recipe using classic Indian spices. Puree the rice for babies under 9 months to avoid choking hazard.

1 tbsp. sunflower oil
1 (1/2-inch) piece gingerroot, peeled and finely chopped
1 clove garlic, peeled and finely chopped
1/2 small onion, peeled and finely chopped
1/2 tsp. ground cumin
1/2 tsp. ground coriander
pinch ground cinnamon

1 boneless, skinless chicken breast, chopped
1 carrot, peeled and chopped
1 (8-oz.) can chopped tomatoes
1/2 cup low-sodium chicken or vegetable stock
1 tbsp. plain full-fat yogurt
1 tbsp. washed and finely chopped
    fresh cilantro

Heat the oil in a nonstick skillet. Blend the ginger, garlic, and onion in a food processor. Add a tablespoon of water if the paste is very thick. Transfer to the skillet and cook on medium-low heat for 5 minutes. Stir in the cumin, coriander, and cinnamon. Cook for 2–3 minutes.

Stir-fry the chicken in the curry sauce for 3–4 minutes until colored. Add the carrot to the curry along with the tomatoes and stock, reduce to a simmer, and cover. Cook for 15–20 minutes, until the carrots are soft and the chicken cooked through. Puree for babies under 9 months. Just before serving, swirl in the yogurt and sprinkle the cilantro on top.

Discard any uneaten rice. Store the curry in the refrigerator for up to 2 days, or freeze immediately and use within 1 month. To use from frozen, carefully defrost. Heat through fully before serving.
Makes 8 child portions or 2 adult portions

beef stew

see variations page 103

Choose lean cuts of beef or lean ground beef for this stew. Red meat is a good source of easily absorbed iron, which babies need for growth and brain development. This stew freezes well.

1 lb. lean beef, cubed, or lean ground beef
1 tsp. dried mixed herbs

2 carrots, washed, peeled, and chopped
2 potatoes, washed, peeled, and chopped

Place the beef into a saucepan with the herbs, then add enough water to cover. Add the chopped carrots and potatoes to the pan. Cover, bring to a boil, and simmer for 20–25 minutes, or until the meat and vegetables are cooked.

Drain the water and reserve. Puree the beef and vegetables, adding the cooking water as needed to achieve the required consistency. Serve warm.

Store in the refrigerator for up to 2 days. Cool the mixture quickly and refrigerate within 1 hour, or freeze immediately and use within 1 month. To use from frozen, carefully defrost. Heat through fully before serving.

Makes 8–10 child portions

moussaka

see variations page 104

A traditional Greek dish of ground lamb and eggplant, topped with a béchamel sauce.

2 tbsp. sunflower oil, divided
1 onion, peeled and finely chopped
1 carrot, peeled and finely chopped
1 garlic clove, peeled and finely chopped
2/3 lb. lean ground lamb
1 tsp. each fresh oregano & thyme
1/2 tsp. each ground cinnamon & allspice

1 (16-oz.) can chopped tomatoes
1 cup low-sodium lamb or beef stock
1 tsp. tomato paste
1 eggplant, cut into 1/2 inch slices
1 quantity cheese sauce (page 191)
1 egg, beaten

Heat 1 tablespoon oil in a nonstick skillet over medium heat. Sauté the onion, carrot, and garlic until softened. Transfer to a large saucepan with lid. Break up the lamb and add to the skillet with the herbs and spices. Cook for 4–5 minutes, until slightly browned, stirring constantly. Transfer to the saucepan. Over medium heat, mix in the tomatoes and juices, stock, and tomato paste. Bring to a boil. Reduce to a simmer, cover, and cook for 1 hour. Meanwhile, heat the remaining oil in the skillet, and fry the eggplant over medium heat until golden brown. Drain on paper towels. Make the cheese sauce (page 191), add the beaten egg, and mix well. Preheat the oven to 400°F. Place a layer of eggplant in a baking dish, cover with the meat sauce, add the remaining eggplant, and top with cheese sauce. Place into the oven and bake for 45–60 minutes until golden brown. Puree for young babies.

Store in the refrigerator for up to 2 days, or freeze immediately and use within 1 month. To use from frozen, carefully defrost. Heat through fully before serving.

Makes 8 child portions or 2–3 adult portions

apple & mango sorbet

see variations page 105

A sorbet is a water ice rather than an ice cream. This version is made without sugar. It is deliciously refreshing on a hot day and a good way to encourage children to taste different flavors and consume fruit.

1 large mango, peeled and stoned
1/4 cup fresh unsweetened apple juice

Place the mango and apple juice in a blender and puree. To freeze with an ice cream maker: Follow the manufacturer's instructions, then transfer to a freezer container and set in the freezer for 30 minutes to firm up before serving.

To freeze without an ice cream maker: Pour the mixture into a suitable freezer container and place in the freezer. After 1 hour, remove the container, pour the contents into a bowl, and whisk to break down the ice crystals. This step is necessary so that you end up with a smooth texture. Pour the mixture back into the freezer container and freeze. Repeat every hour for the next 4 hours, then the sorbet will be ready to serve.

Store in the freezer for no longer than 1 week. Place the container in the refrigerator 30 minutes before you wish to eat it, as it will be very hard.

Makes 1 quart

baked apples

see variations page 106

This was the first food my daughter tried when I was weaning her. I sat next to her chair eating a baked apple while trying to feed her baby rice. She kept leaning forward trying to reach my spoon. I let her try a little of my apple and she loved it. She's a teenager now and still loves baked apples.

6 apples
1 tsp. light brown sugar (optional)

Preheat the oven to 400°F. Wash and core the apples, stuff the sugar into the hollowed-out core (adding the sugar is optional), then score the skin horizontally around the middle. Place in an ovenproof dish and bake for 30–35 minutes, until the apple is soft and the flesh has slightly exploded through the scored skin.

Scoop out the flesh and serve warm or cold. Serve it on its own to a baby, or with a little homemade custard, cream, or ice cream to older children and adults.

Once cool, baked apples can be stored in the refrigerator for 2 days. The mashed flesh can be frozen for up to 1 month. Freeze in ice cube trays until solid, then transfer to a suitable freezerproof container, and label. To defrost, simply remove 2 or 3 cubes of frozen apple mash and let come to room temperature, stir, and serve.

Makes 6–10 child portions

baked bananas

see variations page 107

Bananas can be baked in the oven or grilled outdoors. They are delicious with vanilla ice cream and are just as nice on their own. They are lovely hot or cold.

6 bananas
pinch ground cinnamon
6 tsp. butter

Preheat the oven to 425°F. Slit the banana peel lengthwise on the inside of the curve. Gently ease the banana out, leaving the skin intact. Sprinkle with the cinnamon and dot with the butter.

Put the banana back in the skin and wrap in aluminum foil. Place it directly on the oven rack and bake for 25–30 minutes, until the banana is soft and the skin is blackened. (If the banana is very ripe, reduce the cooking time to 20–25 minutes.)

Scoop out the flesh, mash, and serve. Once cold, store in the refrigerator for 24 hours. The mashed banana can be frozen for up to 1 month. Freeze in ice cube trays until solid, then transfer to a suitable freezerproof container, and label. To defrost, simply remove 2 or 3 cubes of frozen banana mash and let come to room temperature, stir, and serve.

Makes 6–12 child portions

variations

banana yogurt

see base recipe page 53

bananacado yogurt
Prepare the basic recipe, adding 1/2 ripe avocado and mashing it in. Add a little breast milk or formula to achieve the required consistency.

banapple yogurt
Prepare the basic recipe, adding 1 tablespoon apple puree (page 30).

blueberry yogurt pudding
Lightly cook 1 tablespoon fresh or thawed frozen blueberries in a little water for 5 minutes until they collapse. Puree and press through a sieve, then stir into the mashed banana before mixing with the yogurt.

melonana pudding
Prepare the basic recipe, adding 1 pureed slice of peeled ripe cantaloupe or Galia melon.

peachy pudding
Prepare the basic recipe, adding 1 washed, peeled, pitted, and pureed ripe peach.

variations

scrambled eggs

see base recipe page 54

scrambled eggs with cheese
Prepare the basic recipe, adding 1/4 cup finely grated cheddar cheese to the eggs as you beat them with the milk.

scrambled eggs with spinach
Prepare the basic recipe, adding 6–7 chopped fresh baby spinach leaves to the eggs at the start of cooking. The spinach will wilt and cook along with the eggs.

scrambled eggs with pureed vegetables
Prepare the basic recipe, adding a cube (1 tablespoon) of pureed vegetables such as carrots, broccoli, or sweet potato to the scrambled eggs once cooked.

scrambled eggs with salmon
Prepare the basic recipe, adding a tablespoonful of cooked, mashed salmon to the scrambled eggs once cooked.

scrambled eggs with tomato
Prepare the basic recipe, adding 1 fresh tomato. Place the tomato in a bowl, cover it with boiling water, and leave for 10 minutes. The skin will split, making it easy for you to remove it. Remove the skin and seeds, and mash before stirring into the scrambled eggs.

variations

oat porridge

see base recipe page 56

porridge with apple
Prepare the basic recipe. Just before serving, wash, peel, core, and grate 1 apple, and stir it into the cooked porridge.

peachy porridge
Prepare the basic recipe. Stir 1 washed, peeled, pitted, and pureed ripe peach through the cooked porridge with a pinch of ground cinnamon.

porridge with apricot puree
Prepare the basic recipe. Cook 2–3 apricots in a little water for 4–5 minutes until plump, then puree, and add to the porridge.

porridge with raisins
Prepare the basic recipe. Cook 2 teaspoons raisins in a little water until plump, then puree, and add to the cooked porridge.

porridge with pear
Prepare the basic recipe. Just before serving, wash, peel, core, and grate 1 ripe pear, and stir it into the cooked porridge.

variations

baby omelet

see base recipe page 58

herby baby omelet
Prepare the basic recipe. Chop 1 teaspoon fresh herbs and sprinkle them over the omelet before you flip it over.

cheesy baby omelet
Prepare the basic recipe. Sprinkle 1 tablespoon grated hard cheese such as cheddar over the omelet after you've flipped it over.

baby spinach omelet
Prepare the basic recipe, sprinkling 6–7 chopped fresh baby spinach leaves onto the omelet before it sets.

ham & cheese omelet
Prepare the basic recipe. Sprinkle 1 tablespoon grated cheese such as cheddar, and slices of lean wafer-thin ham onto the omelet before it sets. Check that it has thoroughly cooked before folding it over.

baby omelet with pea puree
Prepare the basic recipe, but give it a lovely green sandwich effect. Cook 1/4 cup frozen peas in a little water for 5 minutes until tender, then puree. Spread the pea puree over the cooked omelet before folding it, then cut it into strips.

variations

french toast

see base recipe page 61

french toast with fresh fruit puree
Prepare the basic recipe. Serve with a bit of apple and pear, or apple and mango
puree (see page 45).

french toast with grated cheese
Prepare the basic recipe, adding 1 heaping tablespoon finely grated hard cheese,
such as cheddar, to the egg and milk mixture.

french toast with ham
Prepare the basic recipe. Top the cooked fingers with fingers of lean ham,
and serve.

french toast with herbs
Prepare the basic recipe, adding 1 teaspoon chopped fresh herbs to the egg
mixture before cooking.

french toast with worcestershire sauce (12 months +)
Prepare the basic recipe, adding 1/2 teaspoon Worcestershire sauce to the egg
mixture before cooking. (Worcestershire sauce introduces a new gently spicy
flavor to the baby, but use only a very small amount because it is high in salt.)

variations

spring vegetable soup

see base recipe page 62

spring vegetable soup with potatoes
Prepare the basic recipe, adding 1 peeled and chopped potato to the other
vegetables for a thicker, more filling soup. Puree as before.

spring vegetable soup with peas
Prepare the basic recipe, adding 1 tablespoon fresh or frozen peas in the last
5 minutes of cooking. Peas will sweeten the soup, but it will still have its
"springlike" freshness. Puree as before.

spring vegetable soup with zucchini
Prepare the basic recipe, adding 1 small zucchini, washed and grated, to the
other vegetables. Puree as before.

spring vegetable soup with red bell pepper
Prepare the basic recipe, adding 1 small red bell pepper, chopped, to the other
vegetables. Puree as before.

variations

leek & potato soup

see base recipe page 64

cock-a-leekie
Prepare the basic recipe, adding the chopped meat from 1 chicken thigh to the pan with the potato and leek.

leek & potato soup with carrots
Prepare the basic recipe, adding 1 peeled and chopped small carrot to the pan with the potato and leek.

leek & potato soup with cabbage
Prepare the basic recipe, adding 1/4 head of savoy cabbage to the pan with the potato and leek.

vichyssoise
Prepare the basic soup. Puree and chill it. Serve cold with a little crème fraîche stirred in or swirled on top.

leek & sweet potato soup
Prepare the basic recipe, replacing the potato with one large or two small sweet potatoes.

variations

chicken soup

see base recipe page 67

chicken & corn soup
Prepare the basic recipe, adding 1/2 cup corn kernels (fresh, frozen, or canned) in the last 5 minutes of cooking.

chicken & mushroom soup
Prepare the basic recipe, adding 6 finely chopped button mushrooms with the other vegetables.

chicken noodle soup (12 months +)
Prepare the basic recipe, adding 1 ounce spaghetti broken up into small pieces in the last 10 minutes of cooking time. Make sure the vegetables and chicken flesh are chopped very small, as you don't puree this soup variation so it's not suitable for babies under 12 months.

thai chicken soup (12 months +)
Prepare the basic recipe, adding 2 stalks of fresh lemongrass cut lengthways and 2 kaffir lime leaves, and adding 2 tablespoons fresh or frozen peas and 1 tablespoon fish sauce in the last 5 minutes of cooking.

variations

classic tomato sauce

see base recipe page 69

gazpacho (12 months +)
Prepare the basic recipe and chill completely. Stir in 1/2 finely chopped or grated cucumber, 1/2 finely chopped red or orange pepper, and a pinch of ground cumin and chili powder (optional). Thin the sauce down to a soup consistency by adding 1 cup cold water. Serve with ice cubes floating in each bowl.

tomato dipping sauce
Prepare the basic recipe. After adding the basil, cook the sauce for 20 more minutes until it has thickened, stirring frequently so it does not burn. Serve warm or cold, with vegetable sticks and breadsticks (page 130) for older babies.

tomato soup
Prepare the basic recipe, replace the 1 cup water with 2 cups vegetable stock, puree, and serve warm.

ketchup (12 months +)
Prepare the basic recipe, omitting the basil, and adding a pinch of ground ginger. Cook the sauce without the lid and raise the heat for the last 5 minutes of cooking time to reduce the sauce to a thick, ketchup consistency.

variations

mediterranean roasted vegetables

see base recipe page 70

stuffed eggplants with roasted vegetable sauce
Prepare the basic recipe. Meanwhile, halve 2 eggplants, brush with olive oil, and roast for 30 minutes at 425°F, cut-side down, until soft. Scoop out the flesh, leaving the skin whole. Chop or mash the flesh, mix with half the sauce, and fill the eggplant skins. Sprinkle with a little mozzarella cheese and broil for 3–4 minutes, until the cheese bubbles and starts to brown.

roasted vegetable sauce pasta bake
Prepare the basic recipe and mix with 3/4 pound cooked pasta. Preheat the oven to 375°F, transfer the pasta and sauce to an ovenproof baking dish, sprinkle with grated cheese, and bake for 10 minutes.

roasted vegetable sauce with meatballs
Prepare the basic recipe. Stir in meatballs made from ground beef or lamb (page 208), cook through until piping hot, and serve over pasta.

roasted vegetable sauce on garlic bread (9 months +)
Prepare the basic recipe. Thickly slice some bread, brush with olive oil, and rub with a peeled garlic clove. Toast the bread under the broiler. Place spoonfuls of the sauce on the toasted bread, sprinkle with mozzarella cheese, and serve.

variations

chicken & carrot dinner

see base recipe page 72

chicken, carrot & potato dinner
Prepare the basic recipe, adding 1 peeled and chopped potato.

chicken, carrot & parsnip dinner
Prepare the basic recipe, adding 1 peeled and chopped parsnip.

chicken, sweet potato & spinach dinner
Prepare the basic recipe, adding 1 cup fresh spinach leaves to the chicken and replacing the carrot with 1 steamed or baked mashed sweet potato (page 34).

chicken, lentil & sweet potato dinner (9 months +)
Instead of the basic recipe, put the chopped chicken breast in a pan with 1 washed, peeled, and chopped sweet potato and 1/3 cup red lentils. Cover with water, bring to a boil, and cook for 30–35 minutes. Puree or mash with a little breast milk or formula.

herby chicken dinner
Instead of the basic recipe, put the chopped chicken breast and carrot in a saucepan with 1 peeled and chopped parsnip and potato, and a pinch of dried herbs of your choice. Cover with water, bring to a boil, and simmer for 20–25 minutes. Puree or mash with a little breast milk or formula.

variations

turkey casserole

see base recipe page 75

turkey casserole with mushrooms
Prepare the basic recipe, adding 6 finely chopped mushrooms at the same time as the carrots.

turkey casserole with leeks
Prepare the basic recipe, replacing the onion with 1 washed and finely chopped leek, white part only, at the same time as the carrots.

turkey casserole with potato
Prepare the basic recipe, adding 1 peeled and chopped medium potato at the same as the carrots.

turkey casserole with rutabaga & sweet potato
Prepare the basic recipe, replacing the carrots with 1 small rutabaga and 1 small sweet potato, washed, peeled, and chopped.

turkey casserole with bell pepper
Prepare the basic recipe, replacing the carrots with 2 chopped red or green bell peppers.

variations

beef goulash

see base recipe page 76

beef goulash with rice
Prepare the basic recipe, using 1/4 pound of potatoes, puree and serve the goulash with pureed rice. Leave the dish and rice unpureed for babies over 9 months.

pork goulash
Prepare the basic recipe, replacing the beef with boneless pork.

beef goulash with mushrooms & carrots
Prepare the basic recipe, replacing the green pepper with a few finely chopped mushrooms and 1 washed, peeled, and finely chopped carrot. Puree or mash, and serve as before.

chicken goulash
Prepare the basic recipe, replacing the beef with 2-3 boneless, skinless chicken breasts. Puree or mash and serve as before.

vegetable goulash
Prepare the basic recipe, replacing the beef with 1/2 an eggplant, finely chopped, and replace the beef stock with low sodium vegetable stock. Heat the eggplant in the skillet along with the onion, and prepare as before.

variations

chicken curry with rice

see base recipe page 79

chicken curry with raisins (9 months +)
Prepare the basic recipe, adding 1 tablespoon raisins to the curry at the same time as the stock. Make sure the raisins are mashed or very finely chopped to avoid choking hazard.

cauliflower & potato curry
Prepare the basic recipe, replacing the chicken and carrot with a few washed cauliflower florets and 1 washed, peeled, and chopped small potato. Puree or mash as before.

sweet potato & peas curry
Prepare the basic recipe, replacing the chicken with 1 washed, peeled, and chopped small sweet potato and 1 tablespoon frozen peas. Puree or mash as before.

chicken & mango curry
Prepare the basic recipe, adding 1/2 peeled and chopped ripe mango to the recipe 5 minutes before the end of the cooking time. Puree or mash as before.

beef stew

see base recipe page 80

lamb stew
Prepare the basic recipe, replacing the beef with 1/2 pound of boneless lamb cubes or ground lamb.

pork stew
Prepare the basic recipe, replacing the beef with 1/2 pound of boneless pork cubes or ground pork.

chicken stew
Prepare the basic recipe, replacing the beef with 2–3 boneless, skinless chicken breasts.

beef stew with broccoli & green beans
Prepare the basic recipe. Add 4 broccoli florets and a handful of green beans to the pot with the meat, potato, and carrot during the last 10 minutes of cooking.

beef stew with brown rice
Prepare the basic recipe, omitting the potato. Cook 1/4 cup brown rice in 1/2 cup water for 15–20 minutes, until the water has been absorbed and the rice is tender. Add rice to the beef and carrot, and puree.

variations

moussaka

see base recipe page 83

moussaka with potato slices

Prepare the basic recipe, replacing the eggplant with 3 medium potatoes,
washed, peeled, and cut into thick slices. Puree or mash for younger babies,
or serve as is for babies over 12 months.

beef moussaka

Prepare the basic recipe, replacing the ground lamb with lean ground beef.
Puree or mash, and serve.

vegetable moussaka (9 months +)

Prepare the basic recipe, replacing the meat with 4 ounces green lentils and
adding 1 seeded and finely chopped red pepper to the onion. Puree or mash,
and serve.

turkey moussaka

Prepare the basic recipe, replacing the lamb with ground turkey. Puree or mash,
and serve.

variations

apple and mango sorbet

see base recipe page 84

apple and peach sorbet
Prepare the basic recipe, omitting the mango and using 3 large, ripe, peaches, peeled, pitted, and chopped. Puree the peaches with the apple juice, and freeze.

apple and pear sorbet
Prepare the basic recipe, omitting the mango and using 2 large, ripe, pears, peeled, cored, and chopped. Puree the pears with the apple juice, and freeze.

apple and grape sorbet
Prepare the basic recipe, omitting the mango and using 1 cup seedless grapes, peeled and mashed. Puree the grapes with the apple juice, and freeze.

lime and mango sorbet (12 months +)
Prepare the basic recipe, replacing the apple juice with 1/4 cup freshly squeezed lime juice. If this needs to be sweetened, add a teaspoon of honey.

lemon and mango sorbet (12 months +)
Prepare the basic recipe, replacing the apple juice with 1/4 cup freshly squeezed lemons. If this needs to be sweetened, add a teaspoon of honey.

variations

baked apples

see base recipe page 87

cinnamon-baked apples with frozen yogurt
Prepare the basic recipe, mixing in 1 teaspoon cinnamon with the brown sugar. Serve warm with a scoop of sugar-free frozen yogurt.

baked apples with orange & apricot
Prepare the basic recipe, adding 1 chopped dried apricot to the hollowed-out core. Sprinkle with the grated zest of 1 orange and drizzle with the juice from the orange before baking.

baked apples with pear
Prepare the basic recipe. Mix the brown sugar with the mashed flesh of 1 pear, and stuff it into the hollowed-out core.

baked pears with blueberries
Instead of the basic recipe, core 6 pears, and place in a baking tray. Fill the hollowed-out cores with blueberries. Bake at 400°F for 15–20 minutes. Cool before serving, and puree for young babies.

baked peaches
Prepare the basic recipe, substituting the apple for one large, ripe, stoned peach.

variations

baked bananas

see base recipe page 88

baked bananas with brown sugar and chopped nuts (12 months +)
Prepare the basic recipe, sprinkle a teaspoon of brown sugar on the banana, dot with butter and cook as above, sprinkle with finely chopped/ground nuts to serve.

baked bananas with frozen yogurt
Prepare the basic recipe, serve warm with a scoop of sugar-free frozen yogurt.

baked bananas with chocolate chips (12 months +)
Prepare the basic recipe, replacing the cinnamon and butter with a teaspoon of chocolate chips placed inside the skin next to the banana, serve warm as the chocolate will have melted.

baked bananas with sweetened ricotta cheese
Prepare the basic recipe, mix a teaspoon of icing sugar with a tablespoon of ricotta cheese, serve with the warm banana.

pre-toddler: 9–12 months

Babies are starting to assert their independence,

trying to feed themselves. Milk teeth may be

coming through, making it easier for babies to bite.

It's time to introduce textures, so don't puree their

food quite as much. Be careful of choking hazards

such as whole grapes or berries, and cubes of hard

fruit and vegetables. Enjoy being more adventurous!

potato farls

see variations page 142

This is a good way to use up leftover mashed potatoes. Potato farls are from Ireland and are sometimes known as potato cake or tattie bread. They are a lovely alternative to sandwiches for toddlers. Cut them into small pieces to serve as a snack for babies and toddlers.

4 cups mashed potatoes   2 tbsp. butter, melted
1 cup all-purpose flour

In a large bowl, mix together all the ingredients. Transfer to a lightly floured work surface and knead lightly until everything is well mixed and the mixture is smooth.

With a rolling pin, roll out the mixture into a rough circle about the size of a dinner plate, and cut into quarters (these are the farls), or smaller slices for babies under 12 months.

Heat a heavy-based frying pan over medium–high heat, add a little butter, and swirl it around to coat the bottom of the pan. Place the farls into the hot butter and cook for 3–4 minutes until golden brown. Turn, and cook the other side. Remove from the heat and cover with a clean towel. If covered, they can be kept warm in a low oven for up to 30–40 minutes.

Potato farls are best eaten when warm. If you do want to make them in advance, freeze them as soon as they are cool, defrost thoroughly, and heat through fully before serving. If frozen, use within 1 month.

Makes 8 potato farls

biscotti with babyccino

see variations page 143

Biscotti are very hard, twice-baked Italian biscuits (cookies), which are ideal for dunking in frothy warm milk (a babyccino). For adults, serve with cappuccino or hot chocolate.

1 3/4 cups all-purpose flour
2 tsp. baking powder
1/2 tsp. ground cinnamon
2 eggs, whisked

1 egg yolk
1 tbsp. milk (use breast milk or formula for babies under 12 months)

Preheat the oven to 350°F. Grease and line a baking pan. Mix together the flour, baking powder, and cinnamon in a large bowl. If making for adults, add 3/4 cup sugar to this mixture. Stirring the dry ingredients, add enough egg so that the mixture comes together to form a soft dough. Do not add all the beaten egg, you may not need all of it. If you add too much of the egg, add a little more flour. Split the dough into two pieces, and shape each piece into a log shape. Place the logs on the prepared baking pan and flatten the top of each. Beat together the egg yolk and breast milk/formula for the glaze. With a pastry brush, paint each log with the mixture to glaze. When cooked, the glaze will give the biscotti a shiny finish. Bake the logs for 20–25 minutes until golden brown. Remove from the oven and let cool. Turn the oven down to 325°F. Using a very sharp serrated knife, slice the logs across at 1/2-inch intervals. Lay biscotti on the baking pan, cut-side down, in a single layer. Bake for 15–20 minutes, until dried and golden brown. Remove from the oven and cool on a wire rack.

Keep in an airtight container for up to 1 week, or freeze the day they are made for up to 1 month. If freezing, defrost thoroughly, and heat through fully before serving.

Makes 20–24 biscotti

baby crêpes

see variations page 144

Batter crêpes are delicious with fresh fruit and are very easy to make. Crêpes are ideal finger foods for a baby 9 months and older. Drizzle the crêpes with a little freshly squeezed orange juice.

1/2 cup all-purpose flour
1 egg, beaten

1 cup milk (use breast milk or formula for babies under 12 months)
1 tsp. butter

Place the flour in a bowl, make a well in the center, and pour in the beaten egg. Using a whisk to beat the egg into the flour, start in the middle and gradually add flour from around the edges. Add the milk little by little, making sure you have a smooth batter before adding more. Repeat until all the milk is incorporated.

Melt the butter in a nonstick skillet over medium heat. Pour in enough batter to cover the bottom of the pan. Once the edges begin to lift, turn the crêpe over and cook the other side. Once it starts to bubble, it is ready. Remove to a warm plate, cover with a clean dishtowel or aluminum foil, and repeat until all the batter is used up. Cut into strips for baby. The rest of the family can have big crêpes, make the batter using cow's milk rather than breast milk or formula.

Keep in an airtight container wrapped in plastic wrap for up to 2 days in the refrigerator, or freeze the day they are made for up to 1 month. If freezing, defrost thoroughly, and heat through fully before serving.

Makes 4 crêpes

cheesy mash

see variations page 145

A very adaptable dish to serve with meat, chicken, fish, or just on its own with some fresh vegetables. You could roll the potato mash into 1-inch balls to give to your baby or toddler. If you find the mash is sticky to roll, then dip your fingers in a little flour. Babies love cheesy mash balls.

2 medium potatoes
4 tbsp. grated cheese

Preheat the oven to 425°F.

Prick the potatoes all over using a fork, place on the top rack of the oven and bake for 50–60 minutes until soft in the middle.

Remove from the oven, slit down the middle and scoop out the potato into a bowl. Add the grated cheese and mash, either spoon back into the skin of the potato or serve as it is.

Store in the refrigerator for 3 days, or in the freezer for up to 1 month. Freeze them as soon as they are cool, defrost thoroughly, and heat through fully before serving.

Makes 6–8 portions

oven-baked potato wedges

see variations page 146

Healthier than chips, these are baked in the oven and can be eaten with dips or as a side vegetable. They are a great finger food for 9-month-old babies.

6 large potatoes
6 tsp. sunflower oil

Preheat the oven to 425°F.

Wash and peel the potatoes, cut in half lengthwise, and then into 8–10 wedges, depending on the size of the potato.

Pour the sunflower oil into a freezer-weight bag. Add the potatoes, secure the top, and shake so that the oil coats the potato wedges. (This means that you are adding far less oil than if you drizzled the oil over the wedges on a baking pan.)

Lay the potato wedges on a baking pan and bake for 20–25 minutes, turning halfway through so they cook evenly. They are cooked when golden brown on the outside and soft in the middle. Remove from the oven and let cool a little before serving.

They will keep in the refrigerator for up to 2 days or for up to 1 month in the freezer. If freezing, defrost thoroughly, and heat through fully before serving.

Makes 6–8 portions

dhal

see variations page 147

Lentils are high in protein, low in fat, and contain calcium, iron, and fiber. The baby should have been eating fruit and vegetables for 1–2 months before moving on to lentils. Red lentils are the easiest to digest. Lentils may give your baby gas, so try a small amount of dhal first time. If there are no adverse effects, next time give a little more.

1/4 cup red lentils
1 small onion
a little sunflower oil
3/4-inch piece gingerroot, peeled and grated
1 clove garlic, finely chopped

1/2 tsp. ground coriander
1/4 tsp. ground cinnamon
1/4 tsp. ground turmeric
1 3/4 cups low-sodium vegetable stock

Soak the lentils for 1 hour, drain, rinse, and simmer them in fresh water for 10 minutes, then drain and rinse again, before proceeding with the recipe. Place the lentils in a bowl and cover with water to soak while you prepare the onion. Peel and finely chop or grate the onion. Heat a little sunflower oil in a saucepan, then sauté the onion over a gentle heat for 10–15 minutes until it becomes translucent. Add the gingerroot and garlic, and cook for 1 minute. Add the coriander, cinnamon, and turmeric, and cook for another minute. Drain the lentils, rinse, and add to the pan. Pour in the stock, bring to a boil, cover, and simmer for 20–30 minutes until the lentils are tender. Check on the dhal regularly. If it looks dry, add more stock or water.

Allow to cool slightly and serve, or store in the refrigerator for up to 3 days, or freeze as soon as cooled, for up to 1 month. Defrost thoroughly, and heat through fully before serving.

Makes 6–8 portions

first fish supper

see variations page 148

Fish is a good source of protein, high in vitamins and minerals and quick to cook. Begin with white fish which is mild in flavor such as flounder, lemon sole, cod, and haddock, and gradually introduce stronger tasting oily fish such as salmon, mackerel, and tuna. Oily fish contains high levels of mercury, so should limit your baby's diet to one serving per week. Make sure that all the bones are removed, to avoid choking hazard.

2 boneless flounder fillets
2 cups (or more) milk (use breast milk or
   formula for babies under 12 months)
pinch of dried dill and parsley

2 carrots, peeled and chopped
2 potatoes, peeled and chopped
4 tbsp. finely grated cheddar or Monterey
   Jack cheese

Preheat the oven to 375°F. Place the fish fillets in a shallow ovenproof dish, pour over the milk and sprinkle with the herbs. Cover with aluminum foil and bake for 20–25 minutes, until the fish is cooked.

Bring a pan of water to a boil, add the carrot and potato, and boil for 15 minutes until tender. When the fish is cooked, remove it from the dish and remove the skin. Mash the fish with a little of the milk from the dish. Drain the vegetables and mash them with a little of the milk. Add the grated cheese and mix in. Serve the fish with the mashed cheesy potato and carrot.

Store in the refrigerator for 2 days, or in the freezer for up to 1 month. Freeze as soon as the dish cools, defrost thoroughly, and heat through fully before serving.

Makes 4–6 portions

fish cakes

see variations page 149

Fish cakes made at home are much healthier than store-bought ones. These are particularly healthy because they're baked in the oven instead of fried. Serve with cooked vegetables such as broccoli, chopped up for babies younger than 12 months.

2 large potatoes, peeled and chopped
2 small skinless white fish fillet — cod, haddock, plaice
4 cups milk (use breast milk or formula for babies under 12 months)

2 knobs of butter
4 eggs, beaten
2 cups flour
1 1/2 cup breadcrumbs

Preheat the oven to 350°F. Boil the potatoes in a saucepan for 15–20 minutes, until soft. Meanwhile, place the fillet in an ovenproof dish, cover with milk, and bake for 10–15 minutes, until the fish is cooked through. Remove from the oven and flake the fish, removing all bones. Drain the potatoes and mash with the butter. Add the fish and enough egg to bind the mixture together. You may need only half the egg. Mix well. Form the mixture into balls and flatten them slightly to make small patties. Raise the oven temperature to 400°F. Place the flour in a bowl, the remaining egg in another bowl, and the bread crumbs on a plate. Coat each fish cake in flour, dunk in the egg, and finally in the bread crumbs. Lay the fish cakes on a baking pan, brushed with a little oil. Bake for 10–15 minutes, turning over halfway. Serve.

Store in the refrigerator for up to 2 days, or freeze for up to 1 month. Freeze them as soon as they are cool, defrost thoroughly, and heat through fully before serving.

Makes 12–15 small fish cakes

meatloaf

see variations page 153

A classic meatloaf dish that can be crumbled for baby or sliced as a finger food for a toddler. It's an all-round family favorite.

1 onion, peeled & grated
1 carrot, peeled & grated
1 cup baby spinach, finely chopped
2/3 lb. lean ground beef
1/2 tsp. dried herbs of your choice
pinch ground cinnamon

2 cup bread crumbs
4 tbsp. grated mozzarella cheese
1/2 cup milk (use breast milk or formula for
    babies under 12 months)
1 egg

Preheat the oven to 350°F. In a large bowl, mix all the ingredients together and press into a greased loaf pan. Bake for 1 to 1 1/4 hours until cooked through. Serve warm.

Store in the refrigerator for up to 2 days, or freeze for up to 1 month. Freeze the meatloaf as soon as it is cool, defrost thoroughly, and heat through fully before serving. When reheating, make sure that the center of the meatloaf is hot before serving.

Makes 6–8 child portions or 3–4 adult portions

breadsticks

see variations page 154

This basic bread recipe makes healthy, crunchy breadsticks as well as focaccia (page 215) and a base for pizza (page 211).

2 cups bread flour, plus a little extra
1/2 tsp. salt
1/2 tsp. sugar

1 tbsp. olive oil
1 tsp. quick-rising yeast
3/4 cup warm water

Place the 2 cups of flour, salt, sugar, oil, and yeast in a large bowl, and mix together. Make a well in the center of the flour, pour in half the warm water, and combine with your fingers. Add more water gradually until the mixture forms a dough that is soft and slightly sticky.

Dust a clean work surface with a little flour and tip the dough onto it, sprinkle the dough and your hands with a little flour too.

Transfer the dough to a floured surface and knead for 5–10 minutes until smooth and elastic. Replace in the bowl, cover with plastic wrap or a damp kitchen towel, and leave in a warm place until it has doubled in size. This usually takes about 1 hour.

Preheat the oven to 425°F. Knock the dough back (press out any air bubbles) and break off balls of dough. Roll them into long stick shapes (the width of a pencil and about half as long). Transfer the breadsticks to a greased baking pan, and bake for 10–15 minutes until golden brown. Transfer to a cooling rack to cool. Once cooled, store the breadsticks in an airtight container; they will keep for up to 3 days. Or freeze for up to 1 month.

Makes 8 breadsticks

dried apple rings

see variations page 155

This is a great recipe if you have your own apple tree or if you can buy apples in bulk when they are in season. Soaking apple slices in the lemon juice prevents them from oxidizing and turning brown. The long, slow, cooking process dries out the apples. By removing the water, the apples are preserved, enabling them to keep much longer than fresh apples. Dried apple rings are ideal for babies 9 months old and up to use for teething, and they make a great finger food for toddlers.

10 apples
2 tbsp. lemon juice
3 cups water

Peel, core, and slice the apples into 1/4-inch-thick rings. Combine the lemon juice and water in a bowl. Place the apples into the mixture for 5 minutes, making sure the apples are completely covered. Drain and pat dry.

Preheat the oven to its lowest setting (around 275°F). Lay the apple slices on wire racks or directly on the oven rack. Be certain the racks are very clean. Bake for 1 hour. Check periodically that the apples aren't burning; you want to dry them out rather than cook them. If they start to brown or look like they are cooking rather than drying, turn off the oven and leave them in the oven for 4–5 hours, until they are dry.

When the apples are dry, remove them from the oven and let cool completely. Store in an airtight container for up to 1 month.

Makes 60–70 apple rings

egg-free vanilla ice cream

see variations page 156

Unlike the classic ice cream made with an egg custard base (page 236), this egg-free version of ice cream is just cream and vanilla extract, churned and frozen. Give this only occasionally to your baby as a treat, so that they do not develop a sweet tooth.

2 cups heavy cream
1 cup milk (use breast milk or formula for
    babies under 12 months)

1 1/4 cups granulated sugar
2–3 tsp. vanilla extract

Mix all the ingredients together.

To freeze with an ice cream maker: Follow the manufacturer's instructions, then transfer to a freezer container and set in the freezer for 30 minutes to firm up before serving.

To freeze without an ice cream maker: Pour the mixture into a suitable freezer container and place in the freezer. After 1 hour, remove the container, pour the contents into a bowl, and whisk to break down the ice crystals. This step is necessary so that you end up with smooth ice cream. Pour the mixture back into the freezer container and freeze. Repeat every hour for the next 4 hours, then the ice cream will be ready to serve.

Store in the freezer for no longer than 1 week. Put the container in the refrigerator 30 minutes before you wish to eat it, as it will be very hard.

Makes 1 quart

blueberry jello

see variations page 157

Instead of buying a package of Jell-O, make your own with real fruit juice and fruit, so children are eating food that is good for them as well as being great fun.

4 cups fresh/thawed frozen blueberries
   (including juice)
juice of 2 lemons

4 1/2 cups water
1 packet unflavored gelatin

Place 2 cups of the blueberries in a saucepan with the lemon juice and 1/2 cup water. Slowly bring to a simmer, and then simmer for 5 minutes, until the blueberries collapse. Strain through a fine sieve to remove all the seeds.

Put 4 cups of water into a small bowl, sprinkle in the gelatin, and let soak for 2 minutes, then set it over a bowl of hot water to melt.

Pour the dissolved gelatin into the blueberry juice and stir in the rest of the water.

Place the remaining 2 cups blueberries in the bottom of individual dishes, molds, or in a large bowl. Pour the liquid over the blueberries gently, and let set in the refrigerator for 2–3 hours.

Store in the refrigerator for up to 3 days. Do not freeze.

Makes 4–6 small desserts or 1 adult one

homemade smoothie popsicles

see variations page 158

Basically frozen smoothies, with all the goodness of fresh fruit. Everyone loves these! Don't forget that honey is not safe for babies under 12 months.

4 navel oranges
1 very ripe mango

1 banana
2 tbsp. plain yogurt

Juice the oranges, removing the seeds. Peel, pit, and chop the mango. Peel the banana and chop.

Place the orange juice, mango and banana pieces, yogurt, and honey (if using) into a blender. Puree until smooth. Add a little more orange juice or pineapple juice if the mixture is very thick. Pour into ice pop molds and freeze overnight.

Store in the freezer for up to 1 month.

Makes 5–6 popsicles

apple crumble

see variations page 159

A classic dessert that will appeal to all ages, this recipe will make enough for the whole family, and is just as good the second day. It is delicious served with cream, ice cream, or custard (serve plain for baby).

2 cups self-rising flour
1/2 cup (1 stick) butter or margarine
1/4 cup light brown sugar

1 1/2 lbs. apples, washed, peeled, cored,
  and chopped

Preheat the oven to 400°F. Lightly grease an ovenproof baking dish (about 8 or 9 inches in diameter).

With your fingertips, rub in the flour and butter until it resembles bread crumbs. Stir in the brown sugar.

Layer the apples in the prepared baking dish. Spoon the crumble mixture over the apples and bake for 20–25 minutes, until the crumble topping is golden brown and the apples are soft. For a baby under 12 months, mash the cooked apples a little before serving. Serve warm or cold.

Store in the refrigerator for up to 3 days or in the freezer for up to 1 month. After freezing, heat through fully before serving.

Makes 8–10 child portions or 4 adult portions

variations

potato farls

see base recipe page 109

whole wheat potato farls
Prepare the basic recipe, replacing the all-purpose flour with whole wheat flour.

sweet potato farls
Prepare the basic recipe, replacing the mashed potatoes with the same amount of mashed sweet potatoes.

potato farls toasted with butter
Prepare the basic recipe. Just before serving, lightly toast the farls under the broiler or in a toaster oven, and serve buttered.

mini potato farls
Prepare the basic recipe, but instead of rolling into one circle, roll up small pieces of the potato mixture into a golfball-size ball, flatten, and then cook as before.

parmesan potato farls
Prepare the basic recipe, adding 1/2 cup finely grated Parmesan cheese to the mixture.

biscotti with babyccino

see base recipe page 111

orange biscotti
Prepare the basic recipe, adding the finely grated zest of 2 oranges to the
dry ingredients.

orange & chocolate chip biscotti
Prepare the basic recipe, adding the finely grated zest of 2 oranges to the dry
ingredients along with 1/2 cup dark chocolate chips.

cinnamon–raisin biscotti
Prepare the basic recipe, adding 1/2 cup raisins and an additional 1/2 teaspoon
cinnamon to the dry ingredients.

apricot–orange biscotti
Prepare the basic recipe, adding the finely grated zest of 2 oranges to the dry
ingredients, along with 3–4 finely chopped dried apricots.

variations

baby crêpes

see base recipe page 112

crêpes with apple & cinnamon
Prepare the basic recipe. Before serving, spread 1 tablespoon apple puree (page 30) over the crêpe, and sprinkle with a pinch of ground cinnamon.

crêpes with apple–apricot puree
Prepare the basic recipe. Chop 2 dried apricots and place in a saucepan with 1/4 cup apple juice. Simmer for 5 minutes until the apricot is soft, mash, and serve on top of the crêpes.

crêpes with mashed banana
Prepare the basic recipe. Mash 1/4 to 1/2 banana and spread over the crêpe before serving.

crêpes with bananas and whipped cream
Prepare the basic recipe. Slice 1/4 banana thinly. Top each crêpe with a few banana slices and 1 tablespoon whipped cream. Fold the crêpe over, and slice for a delicious treat.

whole wheat & oatmeal crêpes (12 months +)
Prepare the basic recipe, but increase the crêpes' fiber content (once the baby is 12 months old) by replacing the all-purpose flour with 1/2 cup whole wheat flour and 1/4 cup quick-cooking rolled oats.

cheesy mash

see base recipe page 115

cheesy mash with salmon
Prepare the basic recipe, adding a half fillet of cooked salmon, making sure you remove all the skin and bones, into the cheesy mash.

cheesy mash with chicken
Prepare the basic recipe, shred or chop half a cooked chicken breast into the cheesy mash.

cheesy mash with leeks
Prepare the basic recipe, wash and chop 1/2 a leek, steam for 8-10 minutes until soft and mix with the mash.

orange cheesy mash
Prepare the basic recipe, adding 1 small, cooked carrot to the potato and mash together with the cheese.

cheesy mash with broccoli
Prepare the basic recipe, wash and steam 4-5 florets of broccoli for 5-6 minutes until soft, mash with the cheesy mash, it turns speckled with green bits.

variations

oven-baked potato wedges

see base recipe page 116

oven-baked sweet potato wedges
Prepare the basic recipe, replacing the potato with a sweet potato. Reduce the cooking time by 5 minutes.

oven-baked carrot slices
Prepare the basic recipe, replacing the potato with 1 large carrot, peeled, and sliced.

oven-baked parsnip slices
Prepare the basic recipe, replacing the potato with 1 parsnip, peeled, and sliced.

oven-baked beet slices
Prepare the basic recipe, replacing the potato with 1 beet, peeled, and sliced.

oven-baked eggplant slices
Prepare the basic recipe, replacing the potato with 1 eggplant, peeled, and sliced. Reduce the cooking time by 5 minutes.

variations

dhal

see base recipe page 119

sweet potato dhal
Prepare the basic recipe, adding 1 washed, peeled, and chopped sweet potato at the same time you add the stock.

carrot & cilantro dhal
Prepare the basic recipe, adding 1 washed, peeled, and chopped carrot to the dhal when you add the stock. Add 1 teaspoon finely chopped fresh cilantro just before the end of the cooking time.

chicken dhal
Prepare the basic recipe, adding 1 skinned, chopped chicken breast to the pan at the same time as the spices.

turkey & carrot dhal
Prepare the basic recipe, adding 1/8 pound ground turkey to the pan at the same time as the spices. Add 1 washed, peeled, and chopped carrot when you add the stock.

dhal with cod (or other white fish)
Prepare the basic recipe, adding 1 skinned, deboned, and chopped white fish fillet when you add the stock.

variations

first fish supper

see base recipe page 121

first fish supper with peas
Prepare the basic recipe, omitting the carrots and adding 1 tablespoon fresh or frozen peas to the potato 5 minutes before the end of the cooking time. Puree the peas with the potato. This will make a sweet green mash.

first fish supper with broccoli
Prepare the basic recipe, adding 4 broccoli florets to steam on top of the potato and carrot for 10 minutes, until tender.

first fish supper with beet
Prepare the basic recipe, but replace the carrot with 1 washed, peeled, and chopped beet. This makes a lovely pink mash.

first fish & salmon supper
Prepare the basic recipe, adding 1/2 boneless salmon fillet to the white fish. If baby likes it, then next time replace the white fish with salmon.

first fish supper with sweet potato
Prepare the basic recipe, replacing the potatoes with 2 large sweet potatoes.

variations

fishcakes

see base recipe page 122

fish and sweet potato cakes
Prepare the basic recipe, replacing the potatoes with 2 large sweet potatoes.

fish cakes with pea puree
Prepare the basic recipe. Steam 2 tablespoons peas. When tender, mash with a little crème fraîche, and add to the mashed potato.

fish and carrot cakes
Prepare the basic recipe, replacing 1 potato with 2 large carrots. Peel and chop the carrots, boil them in a saucepan with the potatoes, until soft. Mash with the potato and butter, and prepare as before.

salmon cakes
Prepare the basic recipe, adding 1/2 boneless salmon fillet to the white fish. If baby likes it, then next time replace the white fish with salmon.

tuna cakes
Prepare the basic recipe, adding 1/2 a 5-ounce can of tuna in spring water, drained. If baby likes it, then next time replace the white fish with 1 (5-ounce) can of tuna.

variations

chicken nuggets

see base recipe page 124

herby chicken nuggets
Prepare the basic recipe, adding 1 teaspoon dried tarragon, or other herbs of your choice, to the egg white and cornstarch mixture.

chicken nuggets with bread crumbs
Prepare the basic recipe, replacing the egg white and cornstarch with 1 whole egg, well beaten. After dunking the nuggets into the egg, coat both sides with dried bread crumbs before cooking.

chicken nuggets with cornmeal
Prepare the basic recipe, replacing the egg white and cornstarch with 1 whole egg, well beaten. After dunking the nuggets into the egg, coat both sides with cornmeal, before cooking.

chicken nuggets with crushed chips (12 months +)
Prepare the basic recipe, replacing the egg white and cornstarch with 1 whole egg, well beaten. After dunking the nuggets into the egg, coat both sides with finely crushed unsalted potato chips, before cooking.

variations

beef stroganoff

see base recipe page 125

chicken stroganoff
Prepare basic recipe, replacing the beef with 1 chopped skinless and boneless
chicken breast.

creamy beef stroganoff
Prepare basic recipe, replacing the sour cream with light cream for a
richer version.

beef & mushroom stroganoff
Prepare basic recipe, adding 1/2 cup sliced mushrooms when you start to
cook the steak.

beef stroganoff with mashed potatoes
Prepare basic recipe, replacing the rice with mashed potatoes.

beef stroganoff with noodles
Prepare basic recipe, replacing the rice with noodles such as tagliatelle.

lentil stroganoff
Prepare the basic recipe, replacing the beef with1 cup red lentils. In a saucepan,
cook the lentils for 20 minutes, until tender, and prepare as before.

variations

chilli con carne

see base recipe page 126

lamb chili con carne
Prepare the basic recipe, replacing the ground beef with ground lamb.

turkey chili con carne
Prepare the basic recipe, replacing the ground beef with ground turkey.

vegetable chili
Prepare the basic recipe, replacing the beef stock with vegetable stock, and the ground beef with 1 chopped zucchini, 1 chopped eggplant, and 1/2 pound chopped mushrooms.

three-bean chili
Prepare the basic recipe, replacing the ground beef with two (8-ounce cans) of different beans such as pinto beans, chickpeas, or black beans.

chili con carne with cheesy garlic bread (12 months +)
Prepare the basic recipe. Thinly slice some bread, brush with a little olive oil, and rub with a peeled garlic clove. Sprinkle half a tablespoon of grated mozzarella cheese onto the bread, and toast under the broiler. Serve the chili on the toasted bread, or with the bread on the side.

variations

meatloaf

see base recipe page 129

turkey loaf
Prepare the basic recipe, replacing the ground beef with ground turkey.

chicken loaf
Prepare the basic recipe, replacing the ground beef with ground chicken.

lamb loaf
Prepare the basic recipe, replacing the ground beef with ground lamb.

vegetable loaf
Prepare the basic recipe, replacing the ground beef with 1 cup red lentils and adding 1 (4-oz.) can chopped tomatoes, drained. In a saucepan, cook the lentils, chopped tomatoes, and milk for 20 minutes, until the lentils are tender. Mix with the remaining ingredients and bake for 30–45 minutes, until the top of the loaf looks dry.

variations

breadsticks

see base recipe page 130

bread rolls
Prepare the basic recipe, but split the dough into 6 pieces, roll into balls, and bake as for breadsticks.

whole wheat breadsticks
Prepare the basic recipe, replacing half the bread flour with whole wheat flour.

poppy seed breadsticks (12 months +)
Prepare the basic recipe. Before baking, sprinkle waxed paper with 2 tablespoons poppy seeds. Roll the breadsticks in the seeds before baking.

parmesan breadsticks (12 months +)
Prepare the basic recipe, adding 2 tablespoons finely grated Parmesan cheese to the dry ingredients.

variations

dried apple rings

see base recipe page 132

dried apple rings with cinnamon
Prepare the basic recipe, sprinkling the apple slices with a little ground
cinnamon before putting them into the oven.

dried pear slices
Prepare the basic recipe, replacing the apples with peeled, halved, cored, and
sliced pears. If you want, sprinkle them with a little ground ginger before
putting them into the oven.

dried peach or plum slices
Prepare the basic recipe, replacing the apples with peeled, halved, pitted, and
sliced peaches or plums. If you want, sprinkle them with a little ground
cinnamon before putting them into the oven.

dried apple rings with ricotta cheese
Prepare the basic recipe. To serve, slice the dried rings in half. Serve with
1 tablespoon ricotta cheese as a dip.

rehydrated with golden raisins and yogurt (12 months +)
Prepare the basic recipe, soak the apple rings in water or apple juice for
20–30 minutes, drain, and serve with golden raisins and yogurt.

variations

egg-free vanilla ice-cream

see base recipe page 134

egg-free strawberry ice cream (12 months +)
Prepare the basic recipe, reducing the cream to 1 1/4 cups and omitting the milk and vanilla. Wash, hull, and puree 1 pound strawberries. Pour through a fine sieve to remove the seeds. Mix the puree with the cream and sugar, and freeze.

egg-free blueberry ice cream
Prepare the basic recipe, reducing the cream to 1 1/4 cups and omitting the milk and vanilla. Wash, hull, and puree 1 pound blueberries. Pour through a fine sieve to remove any seeds. Mix puree with the cream and sugar, and freeze.

egg-free chocolate ice cream (12 months +)
Prepare the basic recipe, omitting the vanilla and reducing the cream to 3/4 cup. Warm the milk and cream, and add 1 cup chocolate chips. Stir to melt the chocolate, add the sugar, chill, and freeze.

egg-free banana ice cream
Prepare the basic recipe, reducing the cream to 1 1/4 cups. Puree 2 ripe bananas with the milk, mix with the cream and sugar, and freeze.

egg-free marbled ice cream (12 months +)
Prepare the basic recipe, and the Apple and Mango Sorbet (page 84). Stir the ice cream and sorbet together, creating a ripple effect, then place in the freezer.

variations

blueberry jello

see base recipe page 137

orange jello (12 months +)
Prepare the basic recipe, omitting the blueberries and the lemon juice. Remove the skin and pith from 1 orange and split it into segments. Put the orange pieces in the bottom of the dishes. Reduce the water to 3/4 cup and add 3/4 cup orange juice, freshly squeezed from 5 or 6 oranges.

creamy blueberry jello
Prepare the basic recipe, replacing 3/4 cup of the water with 3/4 cup light cream once the gelatin has been added.

strawberry jello with summer fruit (12 months +)
Prepare the basic recipe, replacing the blueberries with fresh or thawed frozen strawberries, and adding a handful of summer berries to the glasses or mold.

summer berry jello (12 months +)
Prepare the basic recipe, replacing the blueberries with the same quantity of summer berries fresh or thawed frozen, such as blackberries, strawberries, and raspberries.

variations

homemade smoothie popsicle

see base recipe page 138

frozen vanilla smoothie popsicle
Prepare the basic recipe. Replace the plain yogurt with vanilla yogurt.

frozen blueberry smoothie popsicle
Prepare the basic recipe, replacing the mango with 2 cups fresh or thawed frozen blueberries. Puree the berries, then pour through a fine-mesh strainer to remove the seeds before mixing with the other ingredients.

frozen tropical fruit smoothie popsicle
Prepare the basic recipe, adding 1 very ripe small pineapple, peeled, cored, and chopped, and 1 passion fruit, halved, flesh scooped out, and sieved to remove seeds. Add 2 extra tablespoons yogurt. You will make about 10–12 popsicles.

frozen strawberry smoothie popsicle (12 months +)
Prepare the basic recipe, replacing the mango with 1 cup very ripe strawberries. Puree the berries, then pour through a fine-mesh strainer to remove the seeds before mixing with the other ingredients.

frozen mango–raspberry smoothie popsicle (12 months +)
Prepare the basic recipe, adding 1 cup raspberries to the mango. Puree the berries, then pour through a fine-mesh strainer to remove the seeds before mixing with the other ingredients.

variations

apple crumble

see base recipe page 140

apple & pear crumble
Prepare the basic recipe, replacing half the apples with peeled and
chopped pears.

apple & rhubarb crumble
Prepare the basic recipe, replacing half the apples with 1/2 pound
chopped rhubarb.

apple & apricot crumble
Prepare the basic recipe, replacing half the apples with 6 pitted and chopped
fresh apricots.

apple & blueberry crumble
Prepare the basic recipe, replacing half the apples with 2 cups fresh or
thawed frozen blueberries.

peach crumble
Prepare the basic recipe, replacing half the apples with 3 peeled, pitted, and
chopped fresh peaches.

toddler foods:
12 months +

Now's the time to let your little one help with the
cooking. If they can stand unaided and hold a
spoon, they can assist you! Toddlers love stirring —
give them their own bowl to copy you, and
introduce them to a skill that will last a lifetime —
cooking.

breakfast muffins

see variations page 239

The whole wheat flour used in this recipe contains more fiber than white flour. This fiber helps keep children fuller for longer and also helps stave off sugar cravings.

1 cup whole wheat flour
1/2 cup all-purpose flour
2 tsp. baking powder
1 tsp. ground cinnamon
1 tsp. ground ginger
1 cup dark brown sugar

3 carrots, peeled and grated
1 apple, peeled, cored and grated
1 egg
3/4 cup milk
3/4 cup sunflower oil

Preheat the oven to 350°F. Prepare a regular-size muffin pan or a mini-muffin pan with paper baking cups or by greasing the pan. Mix together the flour, baking powder, spices, and sugar. Add the grated carrots and apple and stir to mix.

In a separate bowl, beat the egg, add the milk and sunflower oil, and beat well. Pour mixture into the dry ingredients. Mix well; don't worry if there are any lumps as they will even out during cooking. Evenly fill the muffin cups. Bake regular-size muffins for 15–20 minutes until golden and firm to the touch (10–15 minutes for mini muffins). When a toothpick inserted in the center of a muffin comes out clean, remove the pan from the oven. Let muffins cool before removing from pan.

Store in an airtight container for up to 3 days, or freeze immediately and use within 1 month. To use from frozen, carefully defrost, and heat through fully before serving.

Makes 12 regular or 24 mini muffins

bircher muesli

see variations page 240

Make this traditional Swiss muesli for the whole family. This recipe makes 1 adult serving. For babies between 6 and 9 months, puree it in the food processor.

2 tbsp. quick-cooking rolled oats
a little apple juice (preferably made from fresh apples)

1 apple
1 tbsp. full-fat, plain yogurt

Soak the oats in a little apple juice, just enough to thoroughly moisten them. Let soak for at least 1 hour or overnight.

Wash, peel, core, and grate the apple. Stir pieces through the oats, then stir in the yogurt. Puree if required.

Store in the refrigerator for up to 3 days.

Makes 2–4 portions

granola bars

see variations page 241

These healthy bars are packed full of dried fruit, nuts, and seeds. Do not give these to a baby under 12 months (the maple syrup is not safe for them). These bars are delicious without the nuts, so simply omit for a child with a nut allergy.

6 tbsp. butter
3 tbsp. maple syrup
3 tbsp. fruit spread (such as pear or apricot)
1/2 cup light brown sugar
2 cups old-fashioned rolled oats
   (not quick-cooking oats)

2 tbsp. pecan halves
1/3 cup golden raisins
4 tbsp. mixed seeds, such as sunflower,
   pumpkin, flax, sesame
2 tbsp. ground almonds

Preheat the oven to 350°F. Grease an 8-inch square cake pan with a little butter and line it with waxed or parchment paper. Place the butter, maple syrup, fruit spread, and sugar in a saucepan over medium heat. Heat until the butter has melted and the sugar has dissolved. Stir well to mix. Bring to a boil and cook for 2 minutes until it has a thick, sticky consistency.

Place the remaining ingredients in a large bowl. Pour in the melted ingredients and mix well. Pour into the prepared cake pan, flatten with a wooden spoon, and bake for 15–20 minutes until golden brown. Remove from the oven and leave to cool. Cut into squares.

Keep in an airtight container for 3–4 days, or freeze extra portions the day they are made for up to 1 month. If freezing, defrost thoroughly, let come to room temperature, and serve.

Makes 12–16 bars

cream cheese pinwheels

see variations page 242

Although these can be described as painstaking, the result is usually met by squeals of joy from babies and toddlers, so the effort is worth it.

1 slice thin-sliced bread (or 1 wrap)
cream cheese

If you are using sliced bread, cut off the crusts. Spread a thin layer of cream cheese on one side of the bread or wrap. Roll up tightly so it looks like a log, and secure with a toothpick.

Use a sharp knife to cut 1/2-inch-wide slices from the log. When you turn them on their side, you will see the "pinwheel" effect. Remove the toothpick. Serve immediately, or double-wrap in plastic wrap and refrigerate no longer than 24 hours to prevent pinwheels from drying out.

Makes one portion

lima bean dip with tortilla chips

see variations page 243

Lima beans are a good source of protein, fiber, and magnesium. They can be served as a finger food on their own — just slip off their skins before serving — and they're also good mashed in this lovely dip. Serve in a bowl with tortilla chips. These chips made from tortilla wraps are healthier than store-bought tortilla chips because they are much lower in fat and salt. They're great for small fingers.

1 (8-oz.) can lima beans, drained and rinsed (or
   1 cup frozen lima beans, cooked)
1 tbsp. extra-virgin olive oil
1 garlic clove, peeled and crushed
1 tbsp. plain full-fat yogurt

pinch ground cumin
1 tbsp. washed and chopped fresh flat-leaf
   parsley
1 tortilla, white or whole wheat

To make the dip: Place all the ingredients in a blender or food processor and blend until smooth. Add a little more yogurt or olive oil to achieve a smooth puree. Store in the refrigerator for up to 3 days.

To make the tortilla chips: Heat a skillet until it is hot, add the tortilla, and cook for 3–4 minutes on each side until it is golden brown and crispy. Remove from heat, break into pieces, let cool for a few minutes, and serve on their own or with the lima bean dip.

Makes 4–5 servings of lima dip for every tortilla serving.

tahini dip

see variations page 244

Please note — tahini is made from ground sesame seeds and is not suitable for people suffering from sesame seed allergy. Tahini is a key ingredient in hummus, but it makes a lovely dip on its own. It is especially good with oven-baked potato, eggplant, and zucchini wedges (pages 116 and 146).

1 tbsp. tahini paste
3–4 tbsp. water

Mix the tahini and water together. If it seems a little thick, add a little more water. It can be kept in the refrigerator for 3–4 days.

Makes 4 portions

baby guacamole

see variations page 245

A very easy dip made from a fresh avocado. For younger babies, puree it. For older babies, mash the avocado with a fork. If you make it in advance, quickly cover the bowl with a double layer of plastic wrap to delay the guacamole from turning brown. Because there is lemon juice in the dip, it is not suitable for babies under 12 months. For adults, you may want to add some chili powder or paprika to enhance the flavor.

1 ripe avocado
juice of 1/2 lemon

Halve the avocado, remove the pit, and scoop out the flesh. Puree or mash with the lemon juice and serve with finger foods such as breadsticks (page 130), tortilla chips (page 169), or vegetable sticks such as cucumber and carrot.

Store in the refrigerator for up to 24 hours. The avocado will eventually turn brown, because it oxidizes when it is exposed to air. This will not affect the flavor, however, and the surface can be scraped off easily.

Makes 4 portions

hummus

see variations page 246

Originating in the Middle East, hummus is a dip made from pureed chickpeas. This recipe used canned chickpeas. If you prefer to use dried chickpeas, follow the instructions on the bag precisely, as undercooked beans can be dangerous. If your baby is under 12 months, do not use the tahini. Serve with vegetable sticks, pita bread strips, tortilla chips (page 169), or breadsticks (page 130).

1 (16-oz.) can chickpeas, drained and rinsed
1 tbsp. extra-virgin olive oil
1 garlic clove, peeled and crushed
3 tbsp. plain full-fat yogurt

1 tbsp. tahini paste (optional; omit for sesame seed allergies or for babies under 12 months)

Place all the ingredients in a blender or food processor. Blend until smooth, adding a little more yogurt or olive oil if needed to achieve a smooth puree. Hummus can be stored in an airtight container in the refrigerator for up to 3 days.

Makes 2 cups

mackerel pâté

see variations page 247

Store-bought smoked mackerel fillets make this a quick and easy pâté. Make sure you remove all the bones and the skin. Mackerel is an oily fish that could contain mercury. Therefore we recommend you feed a baby (over 12 months) this recipe and other dishes containing oily fish only on an occasional basis. Despite the mercury content, it's important to remember that oily fish contains many wonderful nutrients for your baby, so it is good that they develop a taste for it. If you wish to make it for adults too, use one fillet per person.

1 mackerel fillet, all bones removed
1 1/2 oz. cream cheese
1 tsp. finely chopped fresh chives

pinch cayenne pepper
grated zest and juice of 1/4 lemon

Flake the mackerel, add the rest of the ingredients, and puree. Cover and refrigerate. Will keep for up to 3 days in the refrigerator.

Makes 2 portions

oatcakes

see variations page 248

These small savory biscuits are ideal for little fingers. These are good as a savory baby biscuit or rusk for teething babies, and are lovely with dips too. They are equally good for adults to eat with cheese.

2 1/2 cups rolled oats
1/4 tsp. baking soda

2 tbsp. white vegetable shortening
1 1/4 cups water

Preheat the oven to 350°F. Place the oats in a food processor and process for 30–60 seconds until the oats resemble a coarse flour. Mix together 2 1/2 cups of the processed oats and baking soda.

Place the shortening in a saucepan with the water. Heat gently until the shortening melts. Add enough of the liquid to the oatmeal mixture to make a firm dough.

Transfer the dough to a piece of waxed or parchment paper. Roll out the dough until it is approximately 1/8 inch thick. Use a round cutter to cut out circles. Place the oatcakes onto a baking sheet lined with parchment paper. Bake for 12–15 minutes.

Remove from the oven and transfer to a cooling rack to completely cool. They can be stored in an airtight container for up to 1 week.

Makes 12 oatcakes

roasted red pepper & tomato soup

see variations page 249

When your baby is 12 months or older, try this soup. It can be served hot or cold. It makes a tasty topping for pizza (page 211), and works well as a pasta sauce. If you are making this for the family, increase the quantities by 3 or 4 times (for a family of 4–5).

2 red bell peppers
8 tomatoes
2 red onions

a little olive oil
5 cups low-sodium vegetable stock

Preheat the oven to 425°F. Wash the red peppers, cut in half, and remove seeds. Cut each half into 3 slices. Wash and halve the tomatoes. Peel the onions and cut into sixths. Lay the peppers, tomatoes, and onions on a greased baking pan. Drizzle with a little olive oil.

Place the pan into the oven and roast for 30–35 minutes, until the peppers are slightly browned at the edges. Transfer the peppers to a plastic freezer-weight bag, tie the top closed, and leave for 5 minutes. The steam from the peppers will make them easy to peel.

Meanwhile, peel the tomatoes and transfer them and the onions to a saucepan with the stock. Untie the bag of peppers and peel off the skin. Add the peppers to the stock. Bring to a boil. Cover and simmer for 30 minutes. Puree.

Freeze extra portions in freezerproof containers, label, and use within 3 months. To use from frozen, carefully defrost. Heat through fully before serving.

Makes 12–16 portions

mini-minestrone

see variations page 250

This lovely hearty soup is great for cold weather. You can use any kind of very small pasta. Cut toast fingers or bread fingers to serve with it. They are lovely to dunk into the soup and eat with your fingers. If you are making this for the whole family, increase the quantities by 3 or 4 times (for a family of 4–5).

2 onions
2 red bell peppers
a little olive oil
1 zucchini
2 carrots, peeled

2 (8-oz.) cans chopped tomatoes, with their juice
3 cups low-sodium vegetable or chicken stock
1/2 cup very small pasta or spaghetti broken into small pieces

Wash, peel, and chop the onions and peppers. Heat the oil in a skillet, add the onion and pepper, and sauté over a gentle heat for 6–7 minutes, until soft. Transfer to a saucepan.

Wash and grate the zucchini and carrots, and add them to the saucepan. Add the stock and canned tomatoes. Bring to a boil. Cover and simmer for 20 minutes.

Return to the pan, add the pasta, and cook for a further 10 minutes, until the pasta is soft.

Freeze extra portions in freezerproof containers, label, and use within 3 months.
To use from frozen, carefully defrost. Heat through fully before serving.

Makes 12–16 portions

fish chowder

see variations page 251

Healthy, filling, and warming, a fabulous recipe for baby and for the rest of the family. If you are making this for the whole family, double the quantities (for a family of 4–5).

2 fillet white fish such as cod, haddock, or
    plaice, skinned and boned
2 medium potatoes
2 carrots

2 small onions
2 tsp. butter
2 tbsp. all-purpose flour
4 cups milk

Cut fish into small pieces and check for any additional bones. Wash, peel, and chop the potatoes, carrots, and onions. If you prefer, you can grate the vegetables instead of dicing, which will give you fewer lumps.

Melt the butter in a frying pan. Add the vegetables and sauté for 5 minutes over low heat. Stir in the flour and mix to coat the vegetables. Pour in half the milk, gradually blending with the floured vegetables. Bring to a boil and simmer for 20–30 minutes, until the potato is tender.

Add the remaining milk and the fish pieces. Continue cooking for 10 minutes more or until the fish is thoroughly cooked. Mash the fish pieces with a fork and serve.

Freeze extra portions in freezerproof containers, label, and use within 3 months. To use from frozen, carefully defrost. Heat through fully before serving.

Makes 6–8 portions

pasta with pea pesto

see variations page 252

All you need to do is cook some fresh or dried pasta, then stir through this lovely creamy sauce to make a fabulous meal. You could serve a bowl of plain cooked pasta to your toddler and give them a spoonful of the sauce for them to mix themselves. For younger babies, use very small pasta shapes and make sure the sauce is well mixed.

1 (10-oz.) package frozen peas, cooked
1/3 cup crème fraîche

1/3 cup fresh mint
finely grated Parmesan, to serve

Place all the ingredients in a food processor or blender and puree. Stir the sauce through hot, cooked pasta and serve with finely grated Parmesan sprinkled on top.

The sauce can be refrigerated for up to 3 days, but not frozen. Crème fraîche does not freeze well.

Makes 4 child portions or 2 adult portions

eggplant bake

see variations page 253

This traditional Italian dish is a firm family favorite. The eggplant soaks up the flavors of the tomato and basil, the cheese melts and it is delicious with lots of crusty bread to soak up the juices.

3 small eggplants
3 tbsp. olive oil
2 1/4 cups grated or torn mozzarella
1/2–1 1/2 cups Classic Tomato Sauce (page 69)

3 tbsp. chopped fresh basil leaves
6 heaping tbsp. grated Parmesan

Preheat the oven to 375°F. Slice the eggplants into 1/2-inch slices. Heat the olive oil in a nonstick skillet and fry the eggplant until golden brown on both sides. Drain on paper towel.

Place half the eggplant slices in a layer in the bottom of a small casserole dish, layer with half the mozzarella, half the tomato sauce, half the basil, and half the Parmesan. Repeat, finishing with the Parmesan.

Bake for 20–30 minutes, until the cheese is golden brown and the dish is bubbling. Serve with green vegetables or a salad and crusty bread.

Store in the refrigerator for up to 2 days or freeze for up to 1 month. Freeze extra portions in small sealable bags or containers, and label. To use from frozen, carefully defrost. Heat through fully before serving.

Makes 6 portions

veggie korma

see variations page 254

Korma is a mild, creamy, curry dish that introduces babies to the flavor of mild spices. Traditionally, this dish includes ground almonds, but I have excluded them from this recipe because of the risk of nut allergies.

1 tbsp. sunflower oil
1 (1/2-inch) piece gingerroot, peeled and finely chopped
1 clove garlic, peeled and finely chopped
1/2 small onion, peeled and finely chopped
1/2 tsp. each ground cumin and coriander
pinch powdered turmeric
1 small potato, peeled and chopped

1 carrot, peeled and chopped
1 tsp. tomato paste
1/2 cup low-sodium vegetable stock
2 tbsp. frozen peas
6–8 broccoli florets
1/2 cup light cream
1 tbsp. finely chopped fresh cilantro
1 cup rice

Heat the oil in a nonstick skillet. Put the gingerroot, garlic, and onion into a food processor and blend to a puree, adding 1 tablespoon water if the mixture is very thick. Add mixture to the skillet and cook on medium–low heat for 5 minutes. Add the spices, and cook for 2–3 minutes. Add the potato and carrot, along with the tomato paste and vegetable stock, reduce to a simmer, cover, and cook for 15–20 minutes, until the vegetables are soft.

Stir in the peas and broccoli florets, and cook for 5 minutes. Stir in the cream and cilantro, and cook for 3–4 minutes. Serve with boiled rice. Store in the refrigerator for up to 3 days or in the freezer for up to 1 month. Freeze extra portions in freezerproof containers, label, and use within 1 month. To use from frozen, carefully defrost. Heat through fully before serving.

Makes 4 child portions or 2 adult portions

macaroni cheese

see variations page 255

This classic childhood dish is a comfort food for toddlers and adults alike. The macaroni is easy for toddlers to pick up with their fingers and great for older toddlers to "hook" onto forks. To make this for babies under 12 months, use breast milk or formula instead of cow's milk.

2 tbsp. butter
2 tbsp. flour
1 cup milk

1/3 cup grated hard cheese such as cheddar
1/4 lb. elbow macaroni
2 tbsp. finely grated Parmesan

To make the cheese sauce: Melt the butter in a saucepan, then add the flour, stirring constantly. Stir for 1–2 minutes to make a smooth roux, then add the milk a little at a time, stirring constantly. Keep adding the milk little by little, making sure it has been absorbed, until the sauce is smooth. When all the milk has been added, stir and gently bring to a boil, which will help thicken the sauce. Just as it reaches a boil, remove the pan from the heat and stir in the grated cheese. Meanwhile, bring a pot of water to a boil, add the macaroni, and cook for 10–15 minutes until al dente. Drain, then return to the pot.

Pour the cheese sauce over the macaroni, transfer to a heatproof dish, sprinkle with the grated Parmesan, and brown under a hot broiler. Serve warm. Mash or puree for babies under 12 months.

Store in the refrigerator for up to 2 days, or freeze extra portions in freezerproof containers, label, and use within 1 month. To use from frozen, carefully defrost. Heat through fully before serving.

Makes 4–6 child portions or 1–2 adult portions

homemade baked beans

see variations page 256

Baked beans are a hugely popular dish, but they can be high in salt and sugar. This homemade version is fabulous, lower in salt and sugar, and extremely tasty as well as easy to make. You can vary the beans or use a mixture of different types. Larger beans such as lima beans can be held as a finger food. For younger babies, you may wish to mash the beans a little to make them safer and easier to swallow. Do not add any salt to the recipe or it will make the beans tough.

1 tbsp. sunflower oil
1 onion
1 cup canned beans (such as butter or small
    white beans), drained and rinsed
1 tsp. powdered mustard

1 tsp. molasses
1 (8-oz.) can chopped tomatoes
1 tbsp. tomato paste
1 tsp. dark brown sugar
1 cup low-sodium vegetable stock

Preheat the oven to 275°F. Heat the oil in a heavy ovenproof dish with a lid. Peel and finely chop the onion, add to the oil, and cook over low heat for 10–15 minutes, until translucent and soft. Add the remaining ingredients, mix well, and bring to a boil. Remove from heat, cover, and transfer to the oven to cook for 4 hours. Stir occasionally while baking.

Store in the refrigerator for up to 3 days, or freeze extra portions in freezerproof containers, label, and use within 1 month. To use from frozen, carefully defrost. Heat through fully before serving.

Makes 8 child portions or 4 adult portions

cauliflower cheese

see variations page 257

Making a cheese sauce to go with vegetables is an easy way to tempt children to eat vegetables. A cauliflower is a lot more tasty with a cheese sauce than on its own, and in England "cauliflower cheese" is a popular comfort food. You can adapt the recipe by adding a little hot sauce to spice up the cheese sauce for adults sharing the meal or by sprinkling some grated Parmesan cheese on the top before broiling.

1 cauliflower, washed and broken into florets
1 quantity cheese sauce (page 191)

Steam the cauliflower over boiling water for 10–15 minutes, until tender. Meanwhile, make the cheese sauce.

Drain the cauliflower, transfer to a heatproof baking dish, and cover with the sauce. Brown for a few minutes under a hot broiler and serve warm. Mash or puree for younger children.

Store in the refrigerator for up to 3 days, or freeze extra portions in freezerproof containers, label, and use within 1 month. To use from frozen, carefully defrost. Heat through fully before serving.

Makes 4–6 baby portions or 2–3 adult portions

family fish pie

see variations page 258

Fish cooked in a creamy cheese sauce with mashed potato topping is a great family meal, packed with vitamins and minerals.

1 lb. firm skinless white fish, such as cod,
   haddock, hake, or pollock
1 cup milk
1 bay leaf
1 pinch dried tarragon and parsley

1 lb. potatoes, peeled and chopped
2 medium carrots, peeled and chopped
1 tsp. butter
1 quantity cheese sauce (page 191), using the
   milk from cooking the fish

Preheat the oven to 350°F. Place the fish into a casserole dish. Cover with the milk and add the bay leaf and herbs. Bake for 30–40 minutes, until the fish is cooked through. Place the potatoes and carrots in a pan of water, bring to a boil, and simmer for 15–20 minutes, until soft. Drain and mash with the butter. Set aside.

Remove the fish from the oven and pour the milk into a measuring cup. Add more milk as needed to measure 1 cup. Make sure all the bones are removed. Flake the fish and return to the casserole dish. Make the cheese sauce (see page 191), using the 1 cup of milk from cooking the fish. Pour the cheese sauce over the fish. Place the potato and carrot mash over the top. Smooth down with a fork, sprinkle with a little grated cheese, and bake for 30–40 minutes until the potato is golden brown and the fish is heated through. Serve warm.

Store in the refrigerator for up to 2 days, or freeze extra portions in freezerproof containers, label, and use within 1 month. To use from frozen, carefully defrost. Heat through fully before serving.

Makes 6–8 child portions or 2–3 adult portions

fish sticks

see variations page 259

Store-bought fish sticks (also known as fish fingers) can be full of additives. If you make them yourself, you know exactly what ingredients have gone into them and you can use the best-quality fish. If you bake them rather than fry, you reduce the amount of fat, making them a lot healthier.

1/2 lb. firm white fish such as cod or haddock, skin and bones removed
1 tbsp. cornstarch or all-purpose flour

1 egg, beaten
2 cups dried bread crumbs
1 tbsp. sunflower oil

Cut the fish into 8–9 finger-size strips. Place the cornstarch, egg, and bread crumbs in three different shallow bowls. Dip each strip of fish into the cornstarch, then the egg, and then the bread crumbs.

To bake: Preheat the oven to 400°F. Place the coated fish sticks onto a baking pan, brushed with a little oil. Cook for 10–15 minutes, turning over halfway, until cooked through and golden brown. Serve with green vegetables, potato wedges (page 116), and homemade tomato sauce (page 69), or ketchup (page 97).

Store in the refrigerator for up to 2 days, or freeze extra portions in freezerproof containers, label, and use within 1 month. To use from frozen, carefully defrost. Heat through fully before serving.

Makes 8–9 fish sticks

moroccan chicken with couscous

see variations page 260

This chicken dish is great with couscous. This dish is great for the whole family to share; just make sure that the chicken is chopped smaller for toddlers than for the adults.

2 onions, peeled and chopped
1 garlic clove, peeled and chopped
1 tbsp. chopped fresh cilantro
1/2 tsp. each ground coriander and cumin
pinch powdered turmeric
juice of 2 lemons
1 tbsp. olive oil

2 skinless, boneless chicken breasts
1 tbsp. sunflower oil
1 carrot, peeled and chopped
about 1 cup low-sodium chicken stock
3 dried apricots, finely chopped
1 tsp. honey

To make the marinade, place half the onion, the garlic, herbs and spices, half the lemon juice, and the olive oil to a food processor. Blend to a puree. Chop the chicken and add to the marinade. Mix well. Marinate for 4 hours or overnight, making sure that the chicken is covered. To cook, heat the oil in a nonstick skillet. Add the chicken with the marinade, and cook over medium heat, stirring, to brown the chicken. Add the carrot and the remaining onion to the skillet, along with enough chicken stock to cover the ingredients. Add the apricots with the honey and remaining lemon juice to the skillet. Bring to a simmer. Cook for 20–30 minutes, uncovered, until the chicken is cooked and the vegetables are soft. Serve.

Store in the refrigerator for up to 2 days. Freeze extra portions in sealable containers, label, and use within 1 month. To use from frozen, carefully defrost. Heat through fully before serving.

Makes 8 child portions or 3–4 adult portions

sweet & sour chicken with rice

see variations page 261

This sweet and sour recipe is very healthy as the meat isn't deep fried. Serve with rice and vegetables — baby corn, green beans, mushrooms, and zucchini all work well.

2 tbsp. sunflower oil
4 skinless, boneless chicken breasts, chopped
2 sweet red peppers, chopped
2 medium carrots, chopped
2 (8-oz.) cans pineapple chunks in juice
2 tsp. soy sauce

2 tbsp. tomato paste
2 tsp. sugar
2 tsp. rice wine vinegar
2 tsp. cornstarch
2 tbsp. water
1 cup rice

Heat the sunflower oil in a wok or large skillet. Stir-fry the chicken, red pepper, and carrot for 5–10 minutes, until the chicken is cooked through and the vegetables are soft.

Cook the rice by placing the rice and water into a small saucepan over medium heat. Bring to a boil, cover, and simmer for 10–15 minutes, until the water has been absorbed and the rice is cooked. Pour the pineapple chunks with the juice into a food processor. Add the soy sauce, tomato paste, sugar, and vinegar. Blend to a smooth puree. Add mixture to the saucepan and stir to mix well with the chicken and vegetables. Mix the cornstarch with the water until smooth, pour into the wok and stir. This will help thicken the sauce. Serve.

Discard any uneaten rice immediately. Store the sweet and sour chicken in the refrigerator for up to 2 days, or freeze extra portions in small sealable containers, label, and use within 1 month. To use from frozen, carefully defrost. Heat through fully before serving.

Makes 6–8 child portions or 2 adult portions

shepherd's pie

see variations page 262

This is a British or Irish meat pie dish made with ground lamb topped with a crust of mashed potato. The term "shepherd's pie" refers to the meat used being lamb.

1 tbsp. sunflower oil
1 onion, peeled and finely chopped
1 carrot, peeled and finely chopped
2/3 lb. lean ground lamb
1 tsp. chopped fresh thyme
pinch ground cinnamon

1 cup low-sodium lamb or beef stock
1 tsp. tomato paste
4 tbsp. frozen peas
1 lb. potatoes, peeled and chopped
2 tbsp. butter
4 tbsp. grated cheddar cheese

Heat the oil in a nonstick skillet over medium heat. Sauté the onion and carrot for 5 minutes, until softened. Transfer to a large saucepan with lid. Break up the lamb and add to the skillet. Cook for 4–5 minutes, stirring often to break the meat into tiny pieces. Transfer to the saucepan, and place over medium heat. Add the thyme, cinnamon, stock, tomato paste, and frozen peas. Bring to a boil. Reduce to a simmer, cover, cook for 30–40 minutes. Cook the potatoes in boiling water for 20 minutes, until soft. Drain, return to the pan, add the butter, and mash. Preheat the oven to 400°F. Transfer the meat mixture to a baking dish. Spread the mashed potatoes evenly over the meat. With a fork, fluff up the potatoes. Sprinkle with cheese and bake for 20–25 minutes, until the cheese has melted and the potato crust is golden brown. Serve.

Store in the refrigerator for up to 2 days, or freeze extra portions in small sealable containers, label, and use within 1 month. Carefully defrost and heat through fully before serving.

Makes 6–8 child portions or 2–3 adult portions

lasagna

see variations page 263

This dish is always a popular family meal. Serve it with a crisp green salad for the adults.

1 tbsp. sunflower oil
1 onion, peeled and finely chopped
1 carrot, peeled and finely chopped
1 sweet red pepper, seeded and finely chopped
1/4 lb. mushrooms, finely chopped
1 lb. lean ground beef

1 (16-oz.) can chopped tomatoes
1 tbsp. tomato paste
1 cup low-sodium beef stock
6–8 fresh lasagna noodles (or use dried)
1 quantity cheese sauce (page 191)
1/3 cup finely grated Parmesan cheese

Heat the oil in a nonstick skillet over medium heat. Add the onion and carrot and sauté for 5 minutes, until softened and starting to brown. Transfer to a large saucepan. Add the pepper and mushrooms to the skillet, and sauté for 2–3 minutes. Transfer to the saucepan.

Break up the beef and add to the skillet. Cook for 4–5 minutes, stirring. Transfer to the saucepan, and place over medium heat and add the chopped tomatoes, paste, and stock. Stir and bring to a boil. Reduce to a simmer, cover, and cook for 30–40 minutes. Puree.

Preheat the oven to 400°F. Cover the bottom of a baking dish with part of the meat sauce, then cover with lasagna noodles. Continue to layer the meat sauce and noodles, finishing with the noodles. Pour the cheese sauce over the noodles, sprinkle with cheese, and bake in the oven for 15–20 minutes until the top is golden brown and the cheese is bubbling.

Store in the refrigerator for up to 2 days. Freeze extra portions in sealable containers, label, and use within 1 month. Carefully defrost and heat through fully before serving.

Makes 8–10 child portions or 3–4 adult portions

beef meatballs

see variations page 264

For younger babies these can be mashed. Once the baby moves on to finger food, these are lovely to hold and nibble. They can be served on their own or with the Classic Tomato Sauce (page 69) or Mediterranean Roasted Vegetables (page 70).

2 lbs. lean ground beef
pinch freshly ground black pepper
3 tbsp. sunflower oil

Preheat the oven to 350°F. Mix the lean ground beef with a pinch of black pepper. Roll the mixture into 1-inch balls.

Heat the oil in a nonstick skillet over medium heat. Carefully fry the meatballs, gently rolling them around the pan, to just sear and lightly color them. Do not allow them to brown, or they will be hard for babies with no teeth to chew.

Transfer to a deep baking pan, cover with aluminum foil, and bake for 10–15 minutes until thoroughly cooked. The foil will prevent the meatballs from browning. Remove from the oven and serve warm.

The meatballs can be refrigerated for up to 2 days or freeze extra portions in freezerproof containers, label, and use within 1 month. To use from frozen, carefully defrost. Heat through fully before serving.

Makes 30–40 meatballs

pizza

see variations page 265

Nothing beats homemade pizza. Using the same bread dough base as you used for breadsticks (page 130), you can make pizza or calzones for the whole family. Let your children, even toddlers, help you. Give them their own ball of dough to knead and roll out, and let them choose their toppings to make their own personal pizza.

for the pizza dough
1 quantity breadstick dough (page 130)

for the topping
1/3 quantity of Classic Tomato Sauce (page 69)
fresh basil leaves
2 cups grated mozzarella cheese

Make the pizza dough. After it has doubled in size, knock back (press out any air bubbles) and divide into 3 or 4 balls.

Preheat oven to 425°F. With a rolling pin, roll out each ball to a circle shape, and top with tomato sauce, fresh basil leaves, and mozzarella cheese. Bake on a nonstick cookie sheet for 15–20 minutes, until the cheese has melted.

Make and freeze extra pizzas in freezerproof containers, label, and use within 1 month. To use from frozen, carefully defrost. Heat through fully before serving.

Makes 3–4 small pizzas

mini quiches

see variations page 266

Quiche is delicious for the whole family. This recipe makes 12 mini quiches.

for the pastry
1 1/2 cups all-purpose flour, plus extra for
    rolling out
4 tbsp. solid white vegetable shortening
4 tbsp. butter
1 tbsp. cold water

for the filling
1/2 cup milk
1 egg
1/2 cup grated cheddar cheese

Preheat the oven to 350°F. Grease a 12-cup mini muffin pan. Rub the vegetable shortening and butter into the flour, using your fingers, until the mixture resembles bread crumbs. Add half the water and mix to make a dough. Add water slowly until the dough comes together.

Dust a clean work surface with a little flour and tip the dough onto it. Sprinkle the dough and your hands with a little flour. With a rolling pin, roll out the dough until it is about 1/4 inch thick. Cut out 12 circles of pastry and press the circles into the cups. Place baking beans on the pastry and bake for 10 minutes, until golden brown. Remove from the oven. Beat the milk and eggs together, add the grated cheese. Pour into the baked crusts. Bake for 15–20 minutes. The pastry should be golden brown and the egg mixture set. Remove from the oven and let cool slightly before serving.

Store in the refrigerator for up to 3 days, or freeze for up to 1 month. Carefully defrost and heat through fully before serving.

Makes 12 mini quiches

focaccia

see variations page 267

This Italian flatbread is easy for little hands to hold, lovely dunked in homemade tomato sauce (see page 69), and great as a base for garlic bread. It's best eaten the same day it is made.

dough for breadsticks (page 130)
olive oil for drizzling

Prepare the dough for breadsticks and let it rise until doubled. Preheat the oven to 425°F.

Knock the dough back (make sure there are no air bubbles) and split into four equal parts. With a rolling pin, roll out each part into an oval, approximately 1/2-inch thick. With your finger, press indentations in the top, then drizzle the top with olive oil.

Place each oval on a greased baking pan and bake for 15–20 minutes until golden brown. Remove and let cool.

Once cooled, store the focaccia in an airtight container for up to 3 days, but note that they are best eaten the same day. Alternatively, as soon as they have cooled, freeze for up to 1 month. To use from frozen, carefully defrost. Heat through fully before serving.

Makes 4 focaccia

cheese biscuits

see variations page 268

This recipe is excellent for making with younger children. Cheese biscuits are lovely eaten warm from the oven, split in half and spread with butter, or eaten cold on a picnic or as part of a packed lunch.

1 cup self-rising flour
2 tbsp. butter
1/2 cup grated cheddar cheese

2 tbsp. milk
1 egg

Preheat the oven to 350°F. With your fingers, rub in the butter into the flour until the mixture resembles bread crumbs. Stir in the grated cheese. Stir in the milk and egg until the mixture forms a dough.

Dust a clean work surface with a little flour and tip the dough onto it. Sprinkle the dough and your hands with a little flour too. Gently flatten the dough with your hands or a rolling pin until it is approximately 1 1/2 inches thick. Use a 3-inch round cookie cutter to cut out the biscuits or cut into 8 wedges with a knife. Reroll and recut any extra dough.

Grease a baking pan and transfer the biscuits onto it. Bake for 12–15 minutes, until they are golden brown and well risen. Once cooled, store the biscuits in an airtight container, but note that they are best eaten the same day. Alternatively, as soon as they have cooled, freeze for up to 1 month. To use from frozen, carefully defrost. Heat through fully before serving.

Makes 4 cheese biscuits

savory cheese muffins

see variations page 269

These make a refreshing change from sandwiches, and are a great recipe for toddlers and children to help you make. Just stirring the mixture will help them feel like they are doing real cooking, and they will be much more willing to try eating the muffins.

1 1/2 cups self-rising flour
1 tsp. baking powder
1 cup grated cheese such as cheddar or
    Monterey Jack

1 egg
3/4 cup milk
5 tbsp. butter, melted

Preheat the oven to 350°F. Prepare a regular-size muffin pan or a mini-muffin pan with paper baking cups or by greasing the pan.

Mix together the flour, baking powder, and grated cheese. Beat the egg, add the milk and melted butter, and beat well. Pour mixture into the dry ingredients. Mix well, but don't worry if there are any lumps, as they will even out during cooking. Evenly fill the muffin cups. Bake regular-size muffins for 15–20 minutes until golden and firm to the touch (10–15 minutes for mini muffins). When a toothpick inserted in the center of a muffin comes out clean, remove the pan from the oven. Let muffins cool before removing from pan.

Once cooled, store the muffins in an airtight container, but note that they are best eaten the same day. Alternatively, as soon as they have cooled, freeze for up to 1 month. To use from frozen, carefully defrost. Heat through fully before serving.

Makes 12 regular or 24 mini muffins

soda bread

see variations page 270

This quick and easy bread uses baking soda and cream of tartar as a rising agent. It's great to use for an emergency alternative to bread and also a good recipe to encourage toddlers to help in the kitchen.

3 cups all-purpose flour, plus a little extra
1 tsp. baking soda
2 tsp. cream of tartar

1/2 tsp. sugar
2 tbsp. butter, melted
1 1/4 cups milk

Preheat the oven to 375°F. Grease a cookie sheet. In a large bowl, mix together the 3 cups flour, baking soda, cream of tartar, and sugar. Make a well in the center of the dry ingredients, and add the melted butter and milk. Use your hands to mix everything together to form a soft dough.

Dust a clean work surface with a little flour and tip the dough onto it. Sprinkle the dough and your hands with a little flour. Divide the dough into 8 lumps for large soda bread or 12 for smaller ones. Leave the lumps rough, as this is how soda bread is meant to look; it's not meant to be rounded. Place the lumps of dough onto the prepared sheet, leaving space around them to expand. Bake for 20–30 minutes until the bread is golden brown.

The bread does not keep very well and is best eaten warm from the oven. It freezes well if frozen on the day it is made, and used within 1 month. To use from frozen, carefully defrost. Heat through fully before serving.

Makes 8 regular or 12 small soda breads

cheddar palmiers

see variations page 271

These cheese pastries are easy to make using ready-made puff pastry. Palmier is French for palm tree, and these pastries are in the shape of a palm leaf or butterfly. They are the same no matter what they are called, and guaranteed to please little ones.

1 sheet prepared puff pastry
1/4 cup finely grated Parmesan cheese

Preheat the oven to 425°F. Grease 1 or 2 cookie sheets. With a rolling pin, roll out the pastry to form a rectangle approximately 4 by 6 inches. Sprinkle 2/3 of the cheese over the pastry, and gently press the cheese into the pastry. Fold over each end to meet in the center of the pastry. Sprinkle the rest of the cheese onto the pastry, then fold (roll) up again. Do not press down on the pastry. This should give you two rolls of pastry that meet in the center.

Use a sharp knife to cut across the rolls into 1/8-inch-wide strips. Lay them on their side on the prepared cookie sheet, leaving space around them to spread. Bake for 8–10 minutes, until golden brown. Transfer to a cooling rack and leave until completely cooled.

Store in an airtight container. They will keep for up to 1 week. If you prefer, the palmiers can be frozen before baking. After cutting them, stack with pieces of parchment or waxed paper between to prevent them from sticking. Freeze for up to 1 month, defrost thoroughly before cooking.

Makes 10–12 palmiers

griddle scones

see variations page 272

These are also known as drop scones (you "drop" spoonfuls of batter onto a hot pan), girdle scones in Scotland (named after the "girdle" they are traditionally cooked on), or blinis. These are a sweet version. They can be given to babies less than 12 months old if you use breast milk or formula instead of cow's milk, and serve plain.

1 1/2 cups self-rising flour
2 eggs

5-6 tbsp. milk (use breast milk or formula for babies under 12 months)
butter for frying

Place the flour in a large bowl. Make a well in the center of the flour, add the eggs, and begin beating with a whisk, gradually taking more flour from around the edges of the well. Add the milk, one tablespoon at a time, whisking it into the flour until you have a soft dropping consistency.

Heat a teaspoon of butter in a skillet set on medium–high heat. Drop tablespoonfuls of the mixture into the pan. You should be able to cook 6 or 7 scones at the same time. Cook for 3-4 minutes. When bubbles form on the surface, turn the scone over. The scone will immediately rise up a little. Cook for another 2-3 minutes, until both sides are golden brown. Remove from the pan. Serve with butter, jam, syrup, lemon juice, or just on their own.

Store for up to 3 days in an airtight container, or they can be frozen for 1 month. To use from frozen, carefully defrost. Heat through fully before serving.

Makes 12 griddle scones

oaty cookies

see variations page 273

These cookies are a great way to encourage your toddler to help you cook. Make sure that the mixture has cooled before letting your toddler roll the mixture into balls and flatten them onto the cookie sheet. With the addition of the oats and raisins, these cookies are slightly healthier than typical cookies.

7 tbsp. butter
4 tbsp. light brown sugar
2 tbsp. maple syrup
3/4 cup self-rising flour

1 1/2 cups quick-cooking rolled oats
1/2 tsp. ground cinnamon
1/2 tsp. ground nutmeg
1/4 cup golden raisins, chopped

Preheat the oven to 400°F. Grease a cookie sheet. Melt the butter, sugar, and syrup in a small saucepan over medium heat. In a bowl, combine the flour, oats, spices, and raisins. Pour in the melted mixture, and mix to a dough.

Place teaspoonfuls of the dough onto the prepared sheet. You should have enough for 12–16 cookies. Gently flatten the tops. Bake for 10–15 minutes until golden brown. Remove from the oven and let cool completely.

Keep in an airtight container for 3–4 days or freeze the day they are made for up to 1 month. To use from frozen, carefully defrost, let come to room temperature, and serve.

Makes 12–16 cookies

fruit muffins

see variations page 274

These muffins contain fresh fruit, making them slightly healthier than plain muffins; however, they are still high in sugar and fat and should be eaten in moderation.

3/4 cup fresh or thawed frozen berries
   (blueberries for babies up to 12 months;
   raspberries, strawberries, and black currants
   for toddlers)
1 1/2 cups self-rising flour

1 tsp. baking powder
3/4 cup light brown sugar
1 egg
3/4 cup milk
1/3 cup butter, melted

Preheat the oven to 350°F. Prepare a regular-size muffin pan or a mini-muffin pan with paper baking cups or by greasing the pan. Wash the berries and remove stems if necessary.

In a bowl, mix together the flour, baking powder, and brown sugar. Add the berries and stir gently to mix. In a separate bowl, beat the egg, add the milk, and beat well. Add the melted butter and stir to combine. Pour mixture into the dry ingredients. Mix well; don't worry if there are any lumps, as they will even out during cooking. Evenly fill the muffin cups. Bake regular-size muffins for 15–20 minutes until golden and firm to the touch (10–15 minutes for mini muffins). When a toothpick inserted in the center of a muffin comes out clean, remove the pan from the oven. Let muffins cool before removing from pan.

Store in an airtight container for up to 3 days or freeze immediately and use within 1 month. To use from frozen, carefully defrost. Heat through before serving if you prefer them warm.

Makes 12 regular or 24 mini muffins

gingerbread men

see variations page 275

Gingerbread men are traditionally made during winter, using warming spices such as ginger, cinnamon, cloves, and nutmeg. This is a good recipe to make with children.

1 1/4 cups all-purpose flour
1 tsp. ground ginger
1/2 tsp. baking soda
4 tbsp. butter
1/2 cup sugar

1 egg yolk
2 tbsp. molasses
2 tbsp. confectioners' sugar
juice of 1/2 lemon
raisins or candy for decoration

Preheat the oven to 350°F. Mix together the flour, ginger, and baking soda. Rub in the butter until the mixture resembles bread crumbs. Stir in the sugar. Mix the egg yolk and molasses together and add to the mixture. Stir to mix, and then use your hands to work into a ball of dough. Sprinkle a little flour onto a clean work surface, and knead the dough until it is smooth. With a rolling pin, roll out the dough until it is 1/4-inch thick. Use a gingerbread man cutter to cut out shapes.

Transfer the gingerbread men to a greased, lined cookie sheet. Bake for 10–12 minutes until golden brown. Remove pan from the oven and leave the gingerbread men for 5–10 minutes to allow them to harden before moving to a cooling rack. Once the cookies have cooled, mix icing using confectioners' sugar and freshly squeezed lemon juice to make a face and clothes on the gingerbread men. Use raisins or candy for buttons.

Place uncooked dough in a freezer bag and freeze for up to 1 month. Cooked gingerbread men can be stored in an airtight container for up to 1 week, or frozen for up to 1 month. To use from frozen, carefully defrost. Heat through before serving.

Makes 12 gingerbread men

thumbprint cookies

see variations page 276

These cookies are a good recipe for older toddlers to help with. They can rub in the fat and flour and stir in the egg, and they can even form the shapes of the cookies. You could use a food processor if you want, but that's no fun for a toddler.

1 1/2 cups self-rising flour
1 stick (8 tbsp.) cold butter
1/2 cup sugar

1 egg
2 tbsp. milk
raspberry jam or jelly

Preheat the oven to 400°F. Grease a cookie sheet. Place the flour and butter in a bowl and rub the flour and butter through your fingers (adding a bit more flour if necessary), until the mixture resembles bread crumbs. Stir in the sugar. Beat the egg and add it to the mixture. Add a little milk at a time, stirring or working with your hands, until you have a soft dough. If the dough is too dry, add a little extra milk.

Place teaspoonfuls of the mixture onto the prepared pan. You should have enough for 12 cookies. The cookies will double in size, so leave space between them. Gently flatten the top and make an indentation with a clean finger in the center. Place a little raspberry jam/jelly into the indentation. Bake for 15–20 minutes until golden brown.

Remove and let cool. Keep in an airtight container for 3–4 days or freeze the day they are made for up to 1 month. Carefully defrost, let come to room temperature, and serve.

Makes 12 cookies

pineapple kebabs with yogurt dip

see variations page 277

These fruity kebabs are gently broiled or grilled to release their juices and flavors. They are a great way to tempt children to try different fruit. Remove the skewers before giving the fruit to toddlers and young children, as they are dangerous.

1/2 pineapple
1/4 cup dark brown sugar
pinch ground cinnamon

juice of 1 lemon or lime
1 tbsp. thick Greek yogurt
1 tsp. honey

Soak 4 bamboo skewers in water for at least 30 minutes. Peel, core, and cut the pineapple into 1-inch chunks.

Mix together the brown sugar, cinnamon, and lemon or lime juice in a saucepan. Cook over low heat, until the sugar dissolves.

Thread the pineapple chunks onto the skewers and brush all over with the sugar mixture. Broil in the oven or cook on a barbecue grill for 3–4 minutes on each side, until the fruit starts to brown. Cut the pineapple pieces smaller if serving to young toddlers.

Mix together the yogurt and honey to serve as a dip with the kebabs.

Store in the refrigerator for up to 3 days.

Makes 4 portions

peach cobbler

see variations page 278

A cobbler is a deep-dish fruit dessert with a biscuit crust. The topping is deliberately left lumpy to achieve the "cobbled" effect that gives the dessert its name. Older toddlers love to help mix the dough. It is lovely served with plain yogurt.

4 ripe peaches, peeled, pitted and chopped
juice of 1 lemon
1 tbsp. granulated sugar
pinch ground cinnamon
1 tbsp. water

for the topping
1 cup flour
1/2 cup cold butter
1/2 tsp. baking powder
1/4 cup granulated sugar
1/2 cup buttermilk
a little brown sugar for sprinkling

Preheat the oven to 350°F. Place the peaches in a saucepan with the lemon juice, sugar, cinnamon, and 1 tablespoon water. Set the pan over low heat and cook for 5 minutes until the peaches are soft. Transfer to a 1 1/2-quart baking dish.

To make the topping, place the flour and butter into a bowl. Rub the butter and flour together, using your fingertips, until the mixture resembles bread crumbs. Stir in the baking powder and sugar. Add the buttermilk. The mixture will be lumpy. Place spoonfuls of the cobbler topping on the peaches. Sprinkle with brown sugar and bake for 20–25 minutes, until golden brown. Serve warm.

Store in the refrigerator for up to 3 days or freeze for up to 1 month. To use from frozen, carefully defrost, heat through fully before serving.

Makes 4–5 child portions or 2 adult portions

chocolate ice cream

see variations page 279

Homemade ice cream tastes much better than store-bought. You do not need an ice cream maker. All you need is a freezer and a lazy day at home to keep churning.

4 egg yolks
1/2 cup sugar
1 cup milk

1 cup semisweet chocolate chips
1 cup heavy cream

Whisk the egg yolks and sugar until they are thick and leave a trail when you remove the whisk. Pour the milk into a saucepan, set over medium heat, and bring it to a boil. As soon as it boils, remove it from the heat. Pour the egg yolk mixture into the hot milk, whisking constantly. Set the saucepan on low heat and stir continuously until the mixture coats the back of the spoon. Do not let it boil, as the mixture will curdle. Remove the pan from the stove, and let cool. In a separate pan, heat the chocolate chips over a low heat until liquid, do not let it bubble. Add the chocolate and the cream to the egg yolk and milk mixture, stirring well. Put it into the refrigerator to chill for around 2 hours until cold.

To freeze with an ice cream maker: Follow the manufacturer's instructions, then transfer to a freezer container and set in the freezer for 30 minutes to firm up before serving.

To freeze without an ice cream maker: Pour the mixture into a suitable freezer container and place in the freezer. After 1 hour, remove the container, pour the contents into a bowl, and whisk to break down the ice crystals. This step is necessary so that you end up with smooth ice cream. Pour the mixture back into the freezer container and freeze. Repeat every hour for the next 4 hours, then the ice cream will be ready to serve. Consume within 1 month.
Makes 1 quart

compote

see variations page 280

A compote usually is made by slowly cooking fresh or dried fruit in a sugar syrup, which may include spices. In this recipe, I have omitted the sugar syrup and substituted apple juice (for babies under 12 months) or orange juice. It can be served warm or chilled, for breakfast with muesli and yogurt or for dessert with yogurt, whipped cream, or ice cream. It is a great way to encourage toddlers to eat fruit.

2 cups dried fruit (such as raisins, apples,
    prunes, figs, cranberries, cherries, apricots)
1 cinnamon stick

3 whole cloves
2 cups orange or apple juice

Place all the ingredients in a small saucepan, set it over medium heat, cover, and cook gently for 15–20 minutes, stirring occasionally, until the fruit is plump. Add a little more juice if the mixture looks like it is drying out.

Remove the cinnamon stick and the cloves. Puree the mixture for young babies. Serve warm or chilled.

Store in the refrigerator for up to 3 days or freeze for up to 1 month. To use from frozen, carefully defrost. Heat through fully before serving.

Makes 4 child portions or 2 adult portions

rhubarb fool

see variations page 281

A fool is traditionally made with cooked, pureed fruit mixed with whipped cream and chilled. This version uses yogurt and crème fraîche, making it a little healthier. Rhubarb is the only vegetable we eat as a fruit. (We eat the stalk of the plant, so it is a vegetable, as fruits contain the seeds of the plant.) Rhubarb can be a little slimy for young palates, so mixing it with the yogurt makes it easier to eat. Hint: For older toddlers, try dunking raw fresh young rhubarb in brown sugar. It has a tangy citrus flavor.

1 cup fresh rhubarb chopped into 1-inch pieces
1 tbsp. light brown sugar
1 tbsp. water

1/2 cup crème fraîche
1/2 cup plain yogurt
1 tbsp. confectioners' sugar

Place the rhubarb in a saucepan along with the brown sugar and water, and simmer for 5–10 minutes, until tender and collapsed. Puree in a blender or food processor.

Whip the crème fraîche and yogurt together, then gently stir in the confectioners' sugar. Stir in the rhubarb puree, transfer to 4 small bowls, chill, and serve.

Store in the refrigerator for up to 3 days, or place extra portions in freezerproof containers and freeze for up to 1 month. To defrost, simply remove from the freezer and let come to room temperature, stir, and serve.

Makes 4 child portions

breakfast muffins

see base recipe page 161

breakfast muffins with dates & apple
Prepare the basic recipe, replacing the carrots with 8 very finely chopped dates.
Reduce the sugar to 1/2 cup.

breakfast muffins with carrots & raisins
Prepare the basic recipe, replacing the apples with 1/4 cup raisins.

breakfast muffins with sweet potato, orange & raisins
Peel, chop, and steam 2 sweet potatoes for 20 minutes until soft, then mash
with a fork. Prepare the basic recipe, adding the sweet potatoes with the grated
zest of 1 orange and 1/4 cup raisins. Mix the juice from the orange with 3/4 cup
confectioners' sugar to make a thin icing to drizzle over each cooled muffin.

breakfast muffins with orange & honey
Prepare the basic recipe, replacing the carrots and apple with the zest and juice
of 2 oranges, and the brown sugar with 3 tablespoons honey.

variations

bircher muesli

see base recipe page 163

bircher muesli with banana
Prepare the basic recipe. Peel and mash 1 banana, and stir it through the muesli just before serving (or pureeing for baby).

bircher muesli with mango
Prepare the basic recipe. Peel and mash 1 ripe mango, and stir it through the muesli just before serving (or pureeing for baby).

bircher muesli with dried fruit
Prepare the basic recipe. Cook 2 dried apricots and 1 tablespoon raisins in a little water for 4–5 minutes, until plump. Puree and add to the muesli.

bircher muesli with pear
Prepare the basic recipe, replacing the apple with 1 washed, peeled, cored, and grated ripe pear.

bircher muesli with berries
Prepare the basic recipe. Squash or mash 1 tablespoon blueberries, and stir them through the muesli just before serving (or pureeing for baby).

variations

granola bars

see base recipe page 164

granola bars with shredded apple
Prepare the basic recipe, adding 1 peeled and finely grated apple to the mixture along with 1/2 teaspoon ground cinnamon.

granola bars with raisins
Prepare the basic recipe, using half golden raisins and half dark raisins.

granola bars with dried apricots
Prepare the basic recipe, using half golden raisins and half finely chopped dried apricots.

granola bars with dried cranberries & hazelnuts
Prepare the basic recipe, replacing the raisins with dried cranberries and the pecans with chopped hazelnuts.

variations

cream cheese pinwheels

see base recipe page 166

cream cheese & jelly pinwheels
Prepare the basic recipe, spreading a thin layer of fruit jelly over the cream cheese before rolling up.

cheesy tomato pinwheels
Prepare the basic recipe, spreading 1/2 teaspoon tomato paste on the cream cheese before rolling up.

guacamole pinwheels
Prepare the basic recipe, replacing the cream cheese with a thin layer of guacamole (page 171).

egg salad pinwheels
Instead of the basic recipe, omit the cream cheese. Hard-boil 1 egg, then mash half the egg with 1 teaspoon mayonnaise. Spread the egg salad thinly on the bread before rolling up.

hummus pinwheels
Prepare the basic recipe, replacing the cream cheese with a thin layer of hummus (page 173).

lima bean dip with tortilla chips

see base recipe page 168

lima bean dip with salmon
Prepare the basic recipe, adding 1 cooked salmon fillet to the blender or food processor.

lima bean dip with chicken
Prepare the basic recipe, adding 1 cooked, chopped chicken breast and 1 additional tablespoon plain yogurt to the blender or food processor.

lima bean dip with lemon & tahini
Prepare the basic recipe, adding the zest and juice of 1 lemon and 1 teaspoon tahini paste to the mixture in the blender or food processor. (Do not use this variation for anyone with sesame seed allergy.)

lima bean dip with lemon & cilantro
Prepare the basic recipe, adding the zest and juice of 1 lemon and replacing the parsley with cilantro.

lima bean dip with sun-dried tomato
Prepare the basic recipe, adding 4 chopped, drained sun-dried tomatoes to the blender or food processor.

variations

tahini dip

see base recipe page 170

lemon tahini dip
Prepare the basic recipe, replacing half the water with the juice of 1 lemon.

tahini & hummus
Prepare the basic recipe, adding 1 tablespoon of your favorite hummus (page 173) to make a tasty thin dipping sauce. This is great for those who prefer thinner dips to hummus.

tahini & paprika dip
Prepare the basic recipe, adding 1/2 teaspoon mild paprika to the dip.

tahini with cumin & coriander dip
Prepare the basic recipe, adding 1/4 teaspoon each of ground cumin and ground coriander.

baby guacamole

see base recipe page 171

lime guacamole
Prepare the basic recipe, replacing the lemon with the juice of 1 lime.

lime & chili guacamole
Prepare the basic recipe, replacing the lemon with the juice of 1 lime and adding a pinch of chili powder.

tomato guacamole
Prepare the basic recipe, adding 1 skinned and finely chopped tomato to the guacamole.

roasted red pepper guacamole
Prepare the basic recipe, adding 1 roasted and pureed red pepper. To roast the pepper, wash and halve it and remove seeds. Cut each half into 3 slices. Bake at 425°F for 30–35 minutes, until the peppers are slightly browned at the edges. Transfer the peppers to a plastic freezer-weight bag, tie the top closed, and leave for 5 minutes. Then remove the skin and puree.

variations

hummus

see base recipe page 173

beet hummus
Prepare the basic recipe, adding 1 washed, peeled, and grated raw beet to the blender or food processor.

roasted onion hummus
Prepare the basic recipe, adding roasted onion to the blender or food processor. To prepare the onion, peel and cut 1 onion into six, drizzle with a little olive oil, and roast on a cookie sheet at 400°F for 20–25 minutes, until soft and slightly brown at the edges.

lemon & cilantro hummus
Prepare the basic recipe, adding the juice of 1 lemon and 1 tablespoon chopped fresh cilantro to the blender or food processor.

roasted red pepper hummus
Prepare the basic recipe, adding 1 roasted and pureed red pepper (see directions page 245, guacamole variation).

sun-dried tomato hummus
Prepare the basic recipe, adding 3–4 chopped, drained sun-dried tomatoes to the blender or food processor.

variations

mackerel pâté

see base recipe page 174

mackerel & tomato pâté
Prepare the basic recipe, adding 1 teaspoon tomato paste.

sardine pâté
Prepare the basic recipe, replacing the mackerel with 1 small can of sardines in tomato sauce. Make sure you first remove the bones.

tuna pâté
Prepare the basic recipe, replacing the mackerel with 1 small can of tuna in water, drained.

salmon pâté
Prepare the basic recipe, replacing the mackerel with 1 cooked salmon fillet or a small can of salmon, drained.

variations

oatcakes

see base recipe page 177

parmesan oatcakes
Prepare the basic recipe, adding 1 tablespoon finely grated Parmesan cheese.

rosemary oatcakes
Prepare the basic recipe, adding 1 teaspoon chopped dried rosemary.

sesame seed oatcakes
Prepare the basic recipe, adding 1 tablespoon sesame seeds (not for anyone with a sesame seed allergy, or for under 12 months).

pumpkin seed oatcakes
Prepare the basic recipe, adding 1 tablespoon pumpkin seeds.

sunflower seed oatcakes
Prepare the basic recipe, adding 1 tablespoon sunflower seeds.

roasted red pepper & tomato soup

see base recipe page 179

roasted red pepper, tomato & zucchini soup
Prepare the basic recipe, adding slices of 1/2 zucchini to the baking pan with the other vegetables.

roasted red pepper & tomato soup with basil
Prepare the basic recipe, adding 1 tablespoon chopped fresh basil to the stock.

roasted red pepper & tomato soup with rice
Prepare the basic recipe. Serve it with rice to make a substantial meal. My son liked this when he was little and named it "ice and soup," because he couldn't pronounce his r's very well.

roasted red pepper & tomato soup with macaroni
Prepare the basic recipe. Stir in some cooked macaroni or other small pasta shapes.

roasted red pepper & tomato soup with sausage balls
Prepare the basic recipe. Roll a little good-quality sausage meat into balls. Place on a cookie sheet and roast in the oven for 15–20 minutes until thoroughly cooked. Serve with the soup.

variations

mini-minestrone

see base recipe page 180

minestrone with rice
Prepare the basic recipe, replacing the pasta with 1/2 cup rice.

minestrone with cheese croutons
Prepare the basic recipe. Cut a few thin slices of cheddar or another hard cheese. Toast bread under the broiler, turn over, lay the cheese on the untoasted side, and toast until the cheese melts and begins to bubble. Cut into fingers or cubes and float on top of each soup serving.

minestrone with meatballs
Prepare the basic recipe. While the soup is cooking, roll 1/3 pound lean ground beef, lamb, or pork into walnut-sized balls. Fry the meatballs in a nonstick skillet for 5-6 minutes, until cooked through. Add the meatballs to the soup just before serving.

minestrone with cabbage
Prepare the basic recipe, replacing the zucchini with 1/4 head chopped savoy cabbage.

minestrone with peas & leeks
Prepare the basic recipe, replacing the zucchini with 1 tablespoon fresh or frozen peas and 1/2 chopped leek (white part).

variations

fish chowder

see base recipe page 183

fish & corn chowder
Prepare the basic recipe, adding 1/2 cup corn kernels (fresh, frozen, or canned)
when you add the fish.

salmon chowder
Prepare the basic recipe, replacing the white fish fillet with a salmon fillet.
(Do not give babies salmon until they have had white fish.)

fish & leek chowder
Prepare the basic recipe, replacing the onion with 1/2 leek.

chicken & corn chowder
Prepare the basic recipe, replacing the fish fillet with 1 chopped chicken breast.
Add the chicken to the soup at the same time as the potatoes. Add 1/2 cup
corn kernels (fresh, frozen, or canned) 5 minutes before the end of the
cooking time.

chicken & sweet potato chowder
Prepare the basic recipe, replacing the fish fillet with 1 chopped chicken breast,
added to the soup at the same time as the potatoes. Replace the potato with
1 small sweet potato.

variations

pasta with pea pesto

see base recipe page 184

pasta with creamy mushroom pasta sauce
Instead of the basic recipe, sauté 2 cups chopped mushrooms and 1/2 onion, sliced, in 1 tablespoon olive oil over medium heat for 5–10 minutes until soft. Puree and mix with 1/3 cup crème fraîche.

pasta with basil pesto
Instead of the basic recipe, place 1 cup fresh basil leaves, 1 tablespoon pine nuts, and 1/2 cup finely grated Parmesan cheese in a food processor. Process to a paste and stir in the crème fraîche.

pasta with red pepper pesto
Instead of the basic recipe, roast 1 sweet red pepper (see directions page 245, guacamole variation). Puree the pulp with 1 tablespoon pine nuts and 1/2 cup finely grated Parmesan cheese. Stir in the crème fraîche.

pasta with sun-dried tomato pesto
Instead of the basic recipe, puree 6 sun-dried tomato halves with 1 tablespoon pine nuts and 1/2 cup finely grated Parmesan. Stir in the crème fraîche.

variations

eggplant bake

see base recipe page 186

eggplant bake with mushrooms
Prepare the basic recipe, adding 4 tablespoons sliced mushrooms in a layer on top of the eggplant.

eggplant bake with chicken
Prepare the basic recipe, adding 1 cooked, sliced chicken breast in a layer on top of the eggplant.

eggplant bake with chicken and mozzarella
Prepare the basic recipe, adding 1 cooked, sliced chicken breast in a layer on top of the eggplant, and replacing the Parmesan with an additional 4 tablespoons mozzarella.

eggplant bake with lentils
Prepare the basic recipe, adding 1 cup cooked puy or green lentils in a layer on top of the eggplant.

variations

veggie korma

see base recipe page 188

vegetable korma with beans
Prepare the basic recipe, replacing the potato with 1/2 cup mixed cooked beans, such as kidney or cannellini.

vegetable korma with sweet potato
Prepare the basic recipe, replacing the potato with 1 small sweet potato.

vegetable korma with chicken
Prepare the basic recipe, replacing the potato with 1 chopped skinless and boneless chicken breast.

vegetable korma with cauliflower
Prepare the basic recipe, replacing the potato with 1/2 cup cauliflower florets. Reduce the vegetable cooking time to 10 minutes.

vegetable korma with zucchini
Prepare the basic recipe, replacing the carrot with 1 zucchini, finely chopped.

vegetable korma with baby spinach
Prepare the basic recipe, adding 1 cup of baby spinach leaves, washed and chopped, when you stir in the cream and cilantro.

variations

macaroni cheese

see base recipe page 191

macaroni cheese with roasted peppers
Prepare the basic recipe, adding 1 roasted red pepper (see directions page 245, guacamole variation), finely chopped or pureed, to the baking dish.

macaroni cheese with sun-dried tomatoes
Prepare the basic recipe, adding 4 drained and finely chopped sun-dried tomatoes to the baking dish.

macaroni cheese with chicken
Prepare the basic recipe, adding 1 cooked and chopped chicken breast to the baking dish.

macaroni cheese with grape tomatoes
Prepare the basic recipe, adding 1/2 cup finely chopped grape tomatoes to the baking dish.

macaroni cheese with roasted eggplant
Prepare the basic recipe, adding 1 chopped and roasted small eggplant to the baking dish. To roast eggplant, wash and chop it, then place on a cookie sheet, drizzle with olive oil, and cook in a hot oven (425°F) for 15–20 minutes, until soft.

variations

homemade baked beans

see base recipe page 192

baked beans & sweet potatoes
Prepare the basic recipe, adding 1 peeled and chopped, large sweet potato 1 hour before the end of the cooking time.

baked beans with meatballs
Prepare the basic recipe. Make 1-inch meatballs from lean ground beef, lamb, or pork (page 208). Add the cooked meatballs to the baked beans just before serving.

spicy baked beans
Prepare the basic recipe, adding 1/2 teaspoon chili powder.

baked beans with sweet potatoes & cheese
Prepare the basic recipe. Place 2 small sweet potatoes into the oven alongside the casserole 90 minutes before the end of the cooking time. Slice the potatoes in half, pour the beans over them, and serve with grated cheddar or Monterey Jack cheese sprinkled over the top.

cauliflower cheese

see base recipe page 194

cauliflower cheese with restuffed potato
Prepare the basic recipe, while baking 1 potato. When the potato is cooked, halve, scoop the flesh from the skin, and mash with a little butter. Replace the mashed potato in the skin and serve with the cauliflower piled on top. For younger children, just mash the potato with a little cauliflower.

cauliflower cheese with mashed sweet potato
Prepare the basic recipe, adding 1 peeled and chopped sweet potato to the steamer with the cauliflower. Once you remove the cauliflower, let the potato steam another 10 minutes. Puree or mash the sweet potato and serve alongside the baked cauliflower, or mash the potato with the cauliflower for younger children.

cauliflower, leek & cheese bake
Prepare the basic recipe, adding 1 washed and chopped leek (white portion) to the steamer with the cauliflower.

cauliflower, leek, carrot & cheese bake
Prepare the basic recipe, adding 2 chopped carrots and 1 chopped leek (white portion) to the steamer with the cauliflower.

variations

family fish pie

see base recipe page 197

fish & salmon pie
Prepare the basic recipe, replacing the white fish with salmon fillet.

fish pie with peas and broccoli
Prepare the basic recipe, adding 1/3 cup frozen peas and 6–8 broccoli florets
to the fish in the casserole dish before you add the cheese sauce.

fish pie with cauliflower
Prepare the basic recipe, adding 6–8 cauliflower florets to the fish in the
casserole dish before you add the cheese sauce.

fish pie with carrot & sweet potato topping
Prepare the basic recipe, replacing the potatoes with sweet potatoes.

fish pie with rosti topping
Prepare the basic recipe, omitting the carrot. Instead of chopping and boiling
the potatoes, wash, peel, and halve them. Boil for 5 minutes, then drain and
coarsely grate them over the fish and sauce in the casserole dish. Top with
bits of butter and the grated cheese before baking.

variations

fish sticks

see base recipe page 198

fish sticks with parmesan
Prepare the basic recipe, adding 1 cup finely grated Parmesan to the bread crumbs.

fish sticks with oats
Prepare the basic recipe, replacing the bread crumbs with 1 cup quick-cooking rolled oats.

batter-fried fish sticks
Prepare the basic recipe, omitting the bread crumbs. Mix the flour and egg together to form a batter. Carefully dip each fish stick into the batter to coat, then cook as before.

fish sticks with crushed chips
Prepare the basic recipe, replacing the bread crumbs with crushed unsalted potato chips.

variations

moroccan chicken with couscous

see base recipe page 201

moroccan lamb
Prepare the basic recipe, replacing the chicken breasts with 10 ounces lean lamb leg steak, chopped.

moroccan vegetables
Prepare the basic recipe, replacing the chicken breasts with 1 (8-ounce) can chickpeas, drained and rinsed; 1 zucchini, washed and chopped; and an extra carrot, washed, peeled, and chopped. Replace chicken stock with vegetable stock.

moroccan chicken with raisins
Prepare the basic recipe, replacing the dried apricots with 2 tablespoons chopped raisins.

moroccan beans
Prepare the basic recipe, replacing the chicken with 1 (8-ounce) can lima beans, drained and rinsed, and 1 (8-ounce) can cranberry (borlotti) beans, drained and rinsed. Replace chicken stock with vegetable stock.

variations

sweet & sour chicken with rice

see base recipe page 202

sweet & sour chicken with noodles
Prepare basic recipe, replacing the rice with 1 nest of egg noodles per person or half a nest (1 ounce) for baby.

sweet & sour pork with rice
Prepare basic recipe, replacing the chicken with 2/3 pound pork tenderloin, chopped.

sweet & sour meatballs with rice
Prepare basic recipe, replacing the chicken with cooked meatballs (page 208).

sweet & sour white fish with rice
Prepare basic recipe, replacing the chicken with 2/3 pound white fish fillet, such as cod, flounder, or halibut. Be sure the skin and all bones are removed. Cook 8–10 minutes.

spicy sweet & sour chicken with rice
Prepare basic recipe, adding 1–2 teaspoons sweet chili sauce to the recipe with the soy sauce.

variations

shepherd's pie

see base recipe page 204

cottage pie
Prepare the basic recipe, replacing the ground lamb with ground beef.

vegetable pie
Prepare the basic recipe, replacing the ground lamb with another peeled and finely chopped carrot, 1 finely chopped zucchini, and 3/4 to 1 pound texturized protein (TVP). Replace the stock with 1 (16-ounce) can chopped tomatoes.

bean & lentil "shepherd's pie"
Prepare the basic recipe, replacing the ground lamb with 1 (8-ounce) can cannellini beans or cranberry (borlotti) beans and 1/2 cup dried red lentils. Replace the stock with 1 (16-ounce) can chopped tomatoes.

shepherd's pie with leek & potato topping
Prepare the basic recipe, replacing 1 large potato with 1 leek (white portion), washed and finely chopped. Steam the leek over the potatoes for the last 10 minutes of cooking. Sprinkled it on the meat before adding the potatoes.

shepherd's pie with sweet potato topping
Prepare the basic recipe, replacing the potatoes with sweet potatoes.

lasagna

see base recipe page 207

spaghetti bolognese
Instead of the basic recipe, make the meat sauce and use it with spaghetti.

lasagna with turkey & cheese sauce
Prepare the basic recipe, replacing the carrot with a few more mushrooms and the ground beef with ground turkey. Replace the tomatoes, tomato paste, and stock with another quantity of cheese sauce. Thin down one portion of cheese sauce with an additional 1 cup milk. Layer and bake as before with the thicker sauce on the top.

vegetable lasagna
Prepare the basic recipe, replacing the ground beef with 1 chopped eggplant and 1 chopped zucchini, and adding another chopped pepper. Preheat the oven to 400°F. Lay the chopped eggplant, zucchini, and pepper on a cookie sheet, drizzle with olive oil, and roast for 20 minutes. Transfer to the saucepan, replace the beef stock with vegetable stock, and add 1 teaspoon each chopped fresh oregano and fresh basil. Continue to cook as before.

lentil & mushroom lasagna
Prepare the basic recipe, replacing the ground beef with 2/3 cup red lentils and doubling the amount of mushrooms. Replace the beef stock with vegetable stock, and cook as before.

variations

beef meatballs

see base recipe page 208

pork & beef meatballs
Prepare the basic recipe, replacing half the ground beef with lean ground pork.

turkey meatballs
Prepare the basic recipe, replacing the ground beef with ground turkey.

lamb meatballs
Prepare the basic recipe, replacing the ground beef with lean ground lamb.

spicy meatballs
Prepare the basic recipe, adding 1/2 teaspoon ground cumin, 1/2 teaspoon ground coriander, and a pinch of cinnamon with the salt and pepper.

beef & carrot meatballs
Prepare the basic recipe, adding 1 small washed, peeled, and finely grated carrot.

variations

pizza

see base recipe page 211

calzone
Prepare the basic recipe, rolling out the dough into 4 circles. Spread a spoonful of tomato sauce on half of each circle, sprinkle with basil leaves, and fold over the other half. Press the edges together, sprinkle with mozzarella, and bake at 425°F for 15–20 minutes, until golden brown.

spinach calzone
Prepare the calzone variation above, but replace the basil with 1/2 cup chopped baby spinach. Sprinkle 1/2 cup grated mozzarella on top of the spinach before folding over the other half of dough. Press the edges of the calzone together, brush with beaten egg, and bake at 425°F for 15–20 minutes, until golden brown.

pizza swirls
Prepare the basic dough recipe, and split the dough into 6–8 pieces. Stretch each piece into a sausage shape, then flatten. Spread sun-dried tomato paste along the flattened side and roll up. Lay the swirls on their side, next to each other, in a greased deep cake pan, with a little space between them. Cover with plastic wrap and leave in a warm place for 30 minutes until they have doubled in size. Bake at 425°F for 10–15 minutes, until golden brown.

variations

mini quiches

see base recipe page 212

salmon mini quiches
Prepare the basic recipe, adding 1/3 cup chopped cooked salmon to the crust before filling with the egg and milk mixture.

broccoli mini quiches
Prepare the basic recipe, adding 1/3 cup cooked broccoli florets to the crust before filling with the egg and milk mixture.

spinach & cheese mini quiches
Prepare the basic recipe, adding 2/3 torn spinach leaves to the crust before filling with the egg and milk mixture, and replacing the cheddar cheese with 1/3 cup crumbled pasteurized feta cheese. Do not use unpasteurized feta for children under 3 years old.

mini quiche lorraine
Prepare the basic recipe, adding 1/3 cup chopped cooked ham or bacon to the crust before filling with the egg and milk mixture.

mushroom & tomato mini quiches
Prepare the basic recipe, adding 1/3 cup chopped mushrooms and 4 skinned, chopped tomatoes to the crust before filling with the egg and milk mixture.

variations

focaccia

see base recipe page 215

sun-dried tomato focaccia
Prepare the basic recipe, adding 3 chopped sun-dried tomatoes to the recipe.

olive focaccia
Prepare the basic recipe, adding 6–8 finely chopped pitted green olives to the recipe.

garlic focaccia
Prepare the basic recipe, replacing the olive oil for drizzling with garlic oil. To make it, very finely chop 1 garlic clove, then pound it with 1 tablespoon olive oil in a mortar with a pestle. Strain, then drizzle over the focaccia just prior to baking.

mozzarella focaccia
Prepare the basic recipe. Before baking the focaccia, drain, then tear a ball of fresh mozzarella cheese into small pieces. Place the cheese pieces in the indentations in the top of the dough.

cherry tomato focaccia
Prepare the basic recipe. Before baking the focaccia, quarter 10 cherry tomatoes and place them in the indentations in the top of the dough.

variations

cheese-biscuits

see base recipe page 216

cheese-biscuit pizzas
Prepare the basic recipe, but split the dough into four equal parts. With a rolling pin, roll each part into a flat circle, top with pizza sauce and the pizza toppings of your choice, sprinkle with mozzarella cheese, and bake for 15–20 minutes, until the cheese has melted and the crust is golden brown and crispy.

plain biscuits
Prepare the basic recipe, omitting the cheese in the base.

cheesy fingers
Prepare the basic recipe. Split the dough into 10 pieces, roll each one into a ball, then flatten and shape into "fingers." Sprinkle each one with a little grated Parmesan and bake for 5–10 minutes.

cheese & sun-dried tomato biscuits
Prepare the basic recipe, adding 1 tablespoon sun-dried tomato paste or 5–6 finely chopped sun-dried tomatoes at the same time as the cheddar cheese.

variations

savory cheese muffins

see base recipe page 217

savory cheese muffins with sun-dried tomato
Prepare the basic recipe, adding 2 tablespoons sun-dried tomato paste to the mixture when you add the egg, milk, and melted butter.

savory olive muffins
Prepare the basic recipe, replacing the cheese with 2 tablespoons finely chopped black or green olives.

savory muffins with pesto & pine nuts
Prepare the basic recipe, replacing the cheese with 2 tablespoons pesto and 1/2 cup pine nuts.

savory muffins with pesto & parmesan cheese
Prepare the basic recipe, replacing the cheese with 2 tablespoons pesto and 2 tablespoons grated Parmesan cheese. Sprinkle a few pine nuts over the top of the muffins before baking.

savory muffins with tapenade
Prepare the basic recipe, replacing the cheese with 2 tablespoons tapenade in any flavor.

variations

soda bread

see base recipe page 218

soda bread with cheese
Prepare the basic recipe, adding 1 1/2 cups grated hard cheese to the dry ingredients. Grate a little cheese on top of each bread just before baking.

soda bread with cheese & chives
Prepare the basic recipe, adding 1 1/2 cups grated hard cheese and chopped fresh chives. Grate a little cheese on top of each bread just before baking.

soda bread with sun-dried tomatoes
Prepare the basic recipe, adding 1/4 cup drained and chopped sun-dried tomatoes with the dry ingredients.

soda bread with sun-dried tomatoes & olives
Prepare the basic recipe, adding 1/4 cup drained and chopped sun-dried tomatoes and 1/4 cup chopped olives with the dry ingredients.

soda bread with sun-dried tomatoes, cheese & seeds
Prepare the basic recipe, adding 1/4 cup drained and chopped sun-dried tomatoes, 1 1/2 cups grated Parmesan cheese, and 3 tablespoons sunflower or pumpkin seeds with the dry ingredients. Grate a little cheese on top of each soda bread and sprinkle with a few seeds just before baking.

variations

cheddar palmiers

see base recipe page 221

cheese straws
Prepare the basic recipe, but sprinkle all the cheese over half of the pastry, fold over, roll out again, and cut into 1/2-inch-wide strips.

sweet cinnamon palmiers
Prepare the basic recipe, replacing the cheese with 1 teaspoon sugar mixed with 1/2 teaspoon ground cinnamon.

pesto palmiers
Prepare the basic recipe, replacing the cheese with 1 tablespoon pesto. Spread 2/3 of the pesto on the pastry and the remaining 1/3 on the rolled-up section as for the cheese version.

cheese & sun-dried tomato palmiers
Prepare the basic recipe, spreading 1 tablespoon sun-dried tomato paste on the pastry before sprinkling on the cheese.

variations

griddle scones

see base recipe page 222

savory cheese griddle scones
Prepare the basic recipe, omitting the sugar and replacing it with 1/4 cup finely grated Parmesan or another hard cheese.

orange griddle scones
Prepare the basic recipe, adding the grated zest and juice of 1 orange and reducing the amount of milk slightly.

raisin griddle scones
Prepare the basic recipe, adding 1 heaping tablespoon raisins with the flour.

apricot griddle scones
Prepare the basic recipe, adding 4–5 chopped, dried apricots with the flour. If you want to give these to a younger baby, chop the apricots very finely and omit the sugar.

chocolate chip griddle scones
Prepare the basic recipe. Once you turn over the griddle scones, sprinkle 4–5 dark chocolate chips onto each one. The chocolate will melt while the griddle scones finish cooking. Serve warm.

oaty cookies

see base recipe page 225

oaty cookies with sunflower seeds
Prepare the basic recipe, adding 1 tablespoon sunflower seeds to the
dry ingredients.

oaty cookies with pumpkin seeds
Prepare the basic recipe, adding 1 tablespoon pumpkin seeds to the
dry ingredients.

oaty cookies with currants
Prepare the basic recipe, replacing the raisins with currants.

oaty cookies with orange
Prepare the basic recipe, adding the finely grated zest of 2 oranges to the dry
ingredients and omitting the nutmeg.

oaty cookies with chopped hazelnuts
Prepare the basic recipe, using half the amount of raisins and the same amount
of chopped hazelnuts. These are not suitable for children and adults with
nut allergies.

variations

fruit muffins

see base recipe page 226

banana muffins
Prepare the basic recipe, replacing the berries with 3 peeled and mashed ripe bananas and 1 teaspoon ground cinnamon.

pear & ginger muffins
Prepare the basic recipe, replacing the berries with 3 peeled, cored, and chopped ripe pears and 1 teaspoon ground ginger.

apple–raisin muffins
Prepare the basic recipe, replacing the berries with 2 peeled, cored, and grated apples, and 1/4 cup raisins.

whole wheat apple–apricot muffins
Prepare the basic recipe, replacing the self-rising flour with 3/4 cup whole wheat flour and an additional 1 teaspoon baking powder. Also, replace the berries with 2 peeled, cored, and grated apples and 1/3 cup chopped dried or fresh peeled apricots.

peach–raspberry muffins
Prepare the basic recipe, replacing the berries with 2 peeled, pitted, and finely chopped peaches and 2 tablespoons raspberries.

gingerbread men

see base recipe page 229

"cinnamen"
Prepare the basic recipe, replacing the ground ginger with 1 1/2 teaspoons ground cinnamon.

gingerbread men with mixed spices
Prepare the basic recipe, adding 1 teaspoon ground cinnamon and 1/2 teaspoon ground cloves to the mixture.

glazed gingerbread men
Prepare the basic recipe. When the gingerbread men have cooled, mix up a thin frosting using confectioners' sugar and freshly squeezed lemon juice. Put the gingerbread men on a cooling rack set over some parchment or wax paper, and drizzle the frosting over them. The paper will catch the drips of frosting and help reduce the amount of clearing up.

gingerbread & raisin cookies
Prepare the basic recipe, stirring half a cup of raisins into the gingerbread mixture. Instead of gingerbread men shapes, make cookies using a cookie cutter.

variations

thumbprint cookies

see base recipe page 230

plain cookies
Prepare the basic recipe, omitting the raspberry jam. You can make these for
9-month-old babies, if they've already had some solid foods, as long as you
use breast milk or formula instead of cow's milk.

currant cookies
Prepare the basic recipe, adding 1/2 cup currants at the same time as the
flour and omitting the raspberry jam/jelly.

orange cookies
Prepare the basic recipe, adding the finely grated zest of 1 orange to the
dough and replacing the raspberry jam/jelly with orange curd.

apple–raisin cookies
Prepare the basic recipe, adding 1 peeled, cored, and grated apple and
1/2 cup raisins at the same time as the flour. Omit the raspberry jam/jelly.

pineapple kebabs with yogurt dip

see base recipe page 233

pineapple & banana kebabs with yogurt dip
Prepare the basic recipe, replacing half the pineapple with 2 bananas, peeled and chopped into chunks. Alternate the banana with the pineapple on the skewers.

pineapple & strawberry kebabs with yogurt dip
Prepare the basic recipe, replacing half the pineapple with 1 cup strawberries, hulled and chopped into chunks. Alternate the strawberries with the pineapple on the skewers.

mixed fruit kebabs with yogurt dip
Prepare the basic recipe, replacing half the pineapple with 1 banana and 1 mango, peeled and chopped into chunks, and 4 strawberries, chopped into chunks. Alternate the different fruit on the skewers.

pineapple kebabs with raspberry & yogurt dip
Prepare the basic recipe. Mash 1/4 cup raspberries and strain to remove the seeds. Swirl into the yogurt dip.

variations

peach cobbler

see base recipe page 234

apple & raspberry cobbler
Prepare the basic recipe, replacing the peaches with 4 apples, washed, peeled, cored, and chopped, and 1/2 cup raspberries.

pear cobbler
Prepare the basic recipe, replacing the peaches with 4 ripe pears, washed, peeled, cored, and chopped.

blueberry cobbler
Prepare the basic recipe, replacing the peaches with 2 cups fresh or thawed frozen blueberries.

rhubarb cobbler
Prepare the basic recipe, omitting the lemon juice and replacing the peaches with 2 cups chopped fresh rhubarb.

chocolate ice cream

see base recipe page 237

mint chocolate ice cream
Prepare the basic recipe, adding 2 teaspoons peppermint extract. If you want your ice cream to be green, add a little green food coloring.

white chocolate ice cream
Prepare the basic recipe, replacing the semisweet chocolate chips with 1 cup melted white chocolate before transferring the churned ice cream to the freezer to solidify.

chocolate chip ice cream
Prepare the basic recipe. Instead of melting the chocolate chips before adding to the mixture, add 1/2 cup white chocolate chips and 1/2 cup milk chocolate chips to the mixture when you start to churn.

toffee ice cream
Prepare the basic recipe, adding 1/2 cup chopped fudge or soft toffee pieces when you start to churn.

strawberry ice cream
Prepare the basic recipe, adding 1 cup chopped fresh strawberries when you start to churn.

variations

compote

see base recipe page 238

rhubarb & ginger compote
Prepare the basic recipe, replacing the dried fruit with 3 cups rhubarb, cut into 1/2-inch pieces, and adding 1 cup brown sugar. Replace the cloves with 1/2 teaspoon ground ginger.

ice cream compote ripple
Prepare the basic recipe, puree the compote, cool, then swirl through slightly softened vanilla ice cream to serve.

apple & apricot compote
Prepare the basic recipe, replacing the dried fruit with 1 cup dried apricots and 3 fresh apples, washed, peeled, cored, and chopped.

apple, pear & plum compote
Prepare the basic recipe, replacing the dried fruit with 1 apple and 1 pear, washed, peeled, cored, and chopped, and 3 plums, peeled, pitted, and chopped.

mixed berry compote
Prepare the basic recipe, replacing the dried fruit with 1 cup raspberries, 1 cup blueberries, and 1 cup hulled and chopped strawberries. Replace the juice with 1/2 cup water.

rhubarb fool

see base recipe page 240

blueberry fool

Prepare the basic recipe, replacing the rhubarb with 1 cup fresh or
thawed frozen blueberries.

apple & cinnamon fool

Prepare the basic recipe, replacing the rhubarb with 3 washed, peeled, cored,
and chopped apples, and 1/2 teaspoon ground cinnamon.

banana & orange fool

Prepare the basic recipe, replacing the rhubarb with 2 mashed bananas and the
zest and juice of 1 orange. Omit the cooking step. Just mix by hand.

berry fool

Prepare the basic recipe, replacing the rhubarb with 1 cup of your favorite fresh
or thawed frozen berries.

index